Learning Single-page Web Application Development

Build powerful and scalable single-page web applications using a full stack JavaScript environment with Node.js, MongoDB, AngularJS, and the Express framework

Fernando Monteiro

PUBLISHING

BIRMINGHAM - MUMBAI

Learning Single-page Web Application Development

Copyright © 2014 Packt Publishing

First published: December 2014

Production reference: 1191214

Published by Packt Publishing Ltd.
Livery Place
35 Livery Street
Birmingham B3 2PB, UK.

ISBN 978-1-78355-209-2

www.packtpub.com

Credits

Author
Fernando Monteiro

Reviewers
Shivang Agarwal
Giacomo Zinetti

Commissioning Editor
Edward Gordon

Acquisition Editor
James Jones

Content Development Editor
Athira Laji

Technical Editor
Vivek Arora

Copy Editors
Simran Bhogal
Ameesha Green
Relin Hedly
Deepa Nambiar

Project Coordinator
Harshal Ved

Proofreaders
Maria Gould
Linda Morris
Jonathan Todd

Indexer
Priya Sane

Graphics
Abhinash Sahu

Production Coordinator
Shantanu N. Zagade

Cover Work
Shantanu N. Zagade

About the Author

Fernando Monteiro is a frontend engineer, speaker, open source contributor, and the mind behind the Responsive Boilerplate, a CSS library built with Less.js for responsive layouts.

He contributes several articles and materials on design, development, and user experience on his blog and for the entire web community.

He is passionate about web standards, frontend development, and mobile design, and he spent the last 12 years creating high-end graphic and web experiences.

He began his career as a graphic designer in 2002 and quickly became an expert in QuarkXPress, producing and editing more than 500 ads, CDs, and DVDs for different companies around the world.

He has also published a book on HTML5 and responsive design for mobile devices: *Instant HTML5 Responsive Table Design How-to*.

Currently, he works as frontend manager in one of the largest private companies in web software development for government institutions. You can find more about him on www.newaeonweb.com.br.

I would like to thank everyone who supported me in this journey. To Ellen, for all the moments of encouragement; my son Mateus, for always being by my side; my mother Paschoalina Patrizzi; and my sister Marcia Monteiro.

I would also like to thank all the team members from Packt Publishing who had direct contact with me and James Jones and Athira Laji for their patience and support.

About the Reviewers

Shivang Agarwal has been working in the web application domain for the past 5 years. So far, he has worked on three different start-ups including one of his own. These products are web applications and are catering to millions of users daily. Being in a start-up for so long has allowed him to experiment with new technologies a lot.

He is a full stack web developer and a product guy. Currently, he is working as a AVP engineer in an e-commerce start-up, Browntape, and leading the technology team there. In the past, he has lead the engineer team of another start-up in the social domain. He has vast experience in SPA development, infrastructure management, and scaling products to cater to millions of users per day.

I would like to thank my parents, Sunil and Manisha Agarwal; my brother and his wife, Shubham and Smoranika Agarwal; and my wife Kriti for their support and patience.

Giacomo Zinetti, also known as Giko, is a full stack web developer from Bregnano, a quiet town near Milan.

Since 1999, he has been passionate about web development, building better websites and applications with innovative user experiences, and cool graphic interfaces, and he's always looking to further the latest technologies.

He likes to work with a team of web enthusiasts, so they can all share their experiences.

He lives life not only through a monitor, but also traveling, taking pictures, juggling, driving (especially motorcycles), snowboarding, playing board games, staying with friends, and playing a new strange sport called tchoukball.

You can find him on Twitter @giacomozinetti or on his website https://giko.it/.

www.PacktPub.com

Support files, eBooks, discount offers, and more

For support files and downloads related to your book, please visit www.PacktPub.com.

Did you know that Packt offers eBook versions of every book published, with PDF and ePub files available? You can upgrade to the eBook version at www.PacktPub.com and as a print book customer, you are entitled to a discount on the eBook copy. Get in touch with us at service@packtpub.com for more details.

At www.PacktPub.com, you can also read a collection of free technical articles, sign up for a range of free newsletters and receive exclusive discounts and offers on Packt books and eBooks.

https://www.packtpub.com/books/subscription/packtlib

Do you need instant solutions to your IT questions? PacktLib is Packt's online digital book library. Here, you can search, access, and read Packt's entire library of books.

Why subscribe?

- Fully searchable across every book published by Packt
- Copy and paste, print, and bookmark content
- On demand and accessible via a web browser

Free access for Packt account holders

If you have an account with Packt at www.PacktPub.com, you can use this to access PacktLib today and view 9 entirely free books. Simply use your login credentials for immediate access.

I would like to dedicate this book to the memory of my father:
José M. Monteiro da Silva 1928-2014 R.I.P.

Table of Contents

Preface

Dynamic web applications and real-time updates with no page refresh, scalable, high performance, and very rich interfaces are increasingly dominating the market for web development today with a new way to develop web content, called Single Page Web Application (SPA). This kind of development allows you to write less server-side code and more client-side code, which is sometimes focused on JavaScript, providing a better user experience with a new way to interact with the application. Products such as Gmail, Trello, and Groupon are examples of successful SPA development.

Throughout the book, we will show important points in the evaluation of the tools/frameworks available in the market for a great user experience with SPA development. Also, we introduce the concept of full-stack applications in JavaScript, using Node.js and MongoDB to build a RESTful API.

How to deal with all of these technologies and get the best out of them all is a very interesting and motivating task. In the course of our book, we will see how to get the best out of this development method, using the latest and greatest technologies to build a sample application.

Enjoy!

What this book covers

Chapter 1, *Understanding Single Page Application*, discusses the main concepts of the MVC pattern applied by different JavaScript libraries as MVC/MVVM/MV*. This chapter gives you an overview of the available tools and the peculiarities of the traditional web application and SPA. Also, we give some tips to choose the best framework for our project.

Chapter 2, Taking a Deep Dive into Node.js and MongoDB, dives into JavaScript on the server side and explains how to run a Node.js server. This chapter then presents the basic concepts such as the event loop, middleware, and Node Package Manager (NPM). We will see how to interact with MongoDB, which is one of the most popular NoSQL databases, using Mongoose ODM (Object Data Modeling) for Node applications.

Chapter 3, API with MongoDB and Node.js, explains how the RESTful API works and the six constraints to consider when creating an API RESTful architecture. We then get our hands dirty with the Express framework, coding the trivial CRUD (Create, Read, Update, Delete) operations for the baseline API.

Chapter 4, Creating a Conference Web Application, shows how to refactor the API using the Yeoman code generator and how to deal with user authentication using the Passport module and some template engines for Node.js to render HTML on the server.

Chapter 5, Starting with AngularJS, covers the core concepts about AngularJS, which is one of the most popular MV* framework, and explains how the framework deals with the MVC pattern, concepts such as two-way data binding, directives, and project organization to prepare the application to scale.

Chapter 6, Understanding Angular Views and Models, unleashes all the power of a generator to build the application scaffold. We will carefully examine the structure of SPA module-wise and rebuild our API using the help of the MEAN.JS generator, which is a powerful tool for creating applications with the MEAN (such as MongoDB, Express, AngularJS, Node.js) stack. We will use the RESTful interface of the WebStorm IDE to test the API.

Chapter 7, Testing Angular SPA with Karma and Protractor, details the basic concepts of tests and implements them using unit testing and e2e testing on SPA, with the help of testing frameworks such as Jasmine, Karma, and Protractor, using WebDriver and Selenium.

Chapter 8, Deploying the Application to the Cloud, takes a look at some important points involving the deploy process of all web applications, such as version control, deployment in the cloud and continuous deployment, and placement of the sample application in production.

What you need for this book

All examples in the book use open source solutions and can be downloaded for free from the links provided in each chapter.

The book's examples use many Node and Grunt modules and some JavaScript libraries, the most current version when writing this book. The examples use Express 4.2.0, a framework for Node. Here is the complete list of modules:

- "body-parser": "~1.2.0"
- "bower": "~1.3.1"
- "compression": "~1.0.1"
- "connect-flash": "~0.1.1"
- "connect-mongo": "~0.4.0"
- "consolidate": "~0.10.0"
- "cookie-parser": "~1.1.0"
- "express": "~4.2.0"
- "express-session": "~1.1.0"
- "forever": "~0.11.0"
- "glob": "~3.2.9"
- "grunt-cli": "~0.1.13"
- "grunt-protractor-webdriver": "^0.1.8"
- "helmet": "~0.2.1"
- "lodash": "~2.4.1"
- "method-override": "~1.0.0"
- "mongoose": "~3.8.8"
- "morgan": "~1.1.0"
- "passport": "~0.2.0"
- "passport-facebook": "~1.0.2"
- "passport-google-oauth": "~0.1.5"
- "passport-linkedin": "~0.1.3"
- "passport-local": "~1.0.0"
- "passport-twitter": "~1.0.2"
- "protractor": "^1.2.0"
- "swig": "~1.3.2"
- "grunt-concurrent": "~0.5.0"
- "grunt-contrib-csslint": "^0.2.0"
- "grunt-contrib-cssmin": "~0.9.0"

- "grunt-contrib-jshint": "~0.10.0"
- "grunt-contrib-uglify": "~0.4.0"
- "grunt-contrib-watch": "~0.6.1"
- "grunt-env": "~0.4.1"
- "grunt-karma": "~0.8.2"
- "grunt-mocha-test": "~0.10.0"
- "grunt-ngmin": "0.0.3"
- "grunt-node-inspector": "~0.1.3"
- "grunt-nodemon": "~0.2.1"
- "grunt-protractor-runner": "^0.2.4"
- "karma": "~0.12.0"
- "karma-chrome-launcher": "~0.1.2"
- "karma-coverage": "~0.2.0"
- "karma-firefox-launcher": "~0.1.3"
- "karma-jasmine": "~0.2.1"
- "karma-phantomjs-launcher": "~0.1.2"
- "load-grunt-tasks": "~0.4.0"
- "should": "~3.3.1"
- "supertest": "~0.12.1"

The following is the list of frontend dependencies:

- "purecss": "~0.5.0"
  - "responsiveboilerplate": "2.3.2"
- "bootstrap": "~3"
  - "angular": "~1.2"
  - "angular-resource": "~1.2"
  - "angular-mocks": "~1.2"
  - "angular-cookies": "~1.2"
  - "angular-animate": "~1.2"
  - "angular-touch": "~1.2"
  - "angular-sanitize": "~1.2"
  - "angular-bootstrap": "~0.11.0"

- ° "angular-ui-utils": "~0.1.1"
- ° "angular-ui-router": "~0.2.10"
- ° "angular-gravatar": "~0.2.1"

You will also need the text editor called WebStorm, which you can download from `http://www.jetbrains.com/webstorm/`.

A modern browser will be very helpful too; we use Chrome, but feel free to use a browser of your choice. We recommend one of these: Safari, Firefox, Chrome, IE, Opera (all in their latest versions).

Who this book is for

If you're new to the world of SPA and want to explore the frameworks and tools available to start building rich SPA, this book is for you. However, if you already have some knowledge in this field, you might want to take a look at *Chapter 7, Testing Angular SPA with Karma and Protractor*, which is about testing a JavaScript MVC application, and *Chapter 8, Deploying the Application to the Cloud*, which is about continuous deployment using integrated cloud services.

You must have a basic to intermediate knowledge of HTML, CSS, and JavaScript to follow the examples in the book, but for some chapters, a slightly more advanced knowledge in web development/RESTful API and Node.js might be required. Don't worry about this; the examples will detail all the code and give you many links to interesting stuff.

Conventions

In this book, you will find a number of styles of text that distinguish between different kinds of information. Here are some examples of these styles, and an explanation of their meaning.

Code words in text are shown as follows: "We can include other contexts through the use of the `include` directive."

A block of code is set as follows:

```
(function() {

  describe('Speakers Controller Tests', function() {
    // Initialize global variables
    var SpeakersController,
```

```
        scope,
        $httpBackend,
        $stateParams,
        $location;
```

When we wish to draw your attention to a particular part of a code block, the relevant lines or items are set in bold:

```
beforeEach(function() {
    jasmine.addMatchers({
        toEqualData: function(util, customEqualityTesters) {
            return {
                compare: function(actual, expected)
```

Any command-line input or output is written as follows:

```
> require("./example.js")
Running through the example
{ greetings: 'Hello Node',
  sayHi: [Function] }
```

New terms and **important words** are shown in bold. Words that you see on the screen, in menus or dialog boxes for example, appear in the text like this: "On your right side, click on your account name right below **Organizations**."

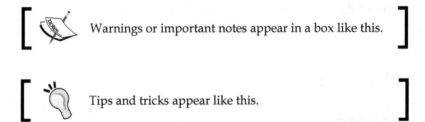

Warnings or important notes appear in a box like this.

Tips and tricks appear like this.

Reader feedback

Feedback from our readers is always welcome. Let us know what you think about this book—what you liked or disliked. Reader feedback is important for us as it helps us develop titles that you will really get the most out of.

To send us general feedback, simply e-mail feedback@packtpub.com, and mention the book's title in the subject of your message.

If there is a topic that you have expertise in and you are interested in either writing or contributing to a book, see our author guide at www.packtpub.com/authors.

Customer support

Now that you are the proud owner of a Packt book, we have a number of things to help you to get the most from your purchase.

Downloading the example code

You can download the example code files from your account at `http://www.packtpub.com` for all the Packt Publishing books you have purchased. If you purchased this book elsewhere, you can visit `http://www.packtpub.com/support` and register to have the files e-mailed directly to you.

Also you can check the book repository on GitHub at: `https://github.com/newaeonweb/conference-api`

Errata

Although we have taken every care to ensure the accuracy of our content, mistakes do happen. If you find a mistake in one of our books—maybe a mistake in the text or the code—we would be grateful if you could report this to us. By doing so, you can save other readers from frustration and help us improve subsequent versions of this book. If you find any errata, please report them by visiting `http://www.packtpub.com/submit-errata`, selecting your book, clicking on the **Errata Submission Form** link, and entering the details of your errata. Once your errata are verified, your submission will be accepted and the errata will be uploaded to our website or added to any list of existing errata under the Errata section of that title.

To view the previously submitted errata, go to `https://www.packtpub.com/books/content/support` and enter the name of the book in the search field. The required information will appear under the Errata section.

Piracy

Piracy of copyrighted material on the Internet is an ongoing problem across all media. At Packt, we take the protection of our copyright and licenses very seriously. If you come across any illegal copies of our works in any form on the Internet, please provide us with the location address or website name immediately so that we can pursue a remedy.

Please contact us at `copyright@packtpub.com` with a link to the suspected pirated material.

We appreciate your help in protecting our authors and our ability to bring you valuable content.

Questions

If you have a problem with any aspect of this book, you can contact us at questions@packtpub.com, and we will do our best to address the problem.

1
Understanding Single Page Application

Single Page Application (SPA) is the greatest sensation at the moment. We have countless JavaScript frameworks available to ease our work. We cannot deny that JavaScript, as just a scripting language, has become the largest technology evolution since the rise of the Web, and of course, the browser's support is much better than the old times. Now, we can use the JavaScript language on both sides, that is, from the frontend to the backend (Node.js) and also include databases with MongoDB (we will talk about them briefly in the next chapters). Now, we focus on understanding the MVC/MVVM pattern on SPA. We will cover the following topics:

- Getting acquainted with SPAs
- Understanding the working of SPAs
- Understanding the MVC/MVVM/MV* pattern
- Peculiarities between SPA and traditional web development
- Choosing a library or framework
- Introducing the MEAN stack
- The available tools
- It's all about JavaScript
- HTML, CSS, and the responsive way

Getting acquainted with SPA

SPA is a web application or website that fits on a single web page with the goal of providing a more fluid user experience and a rich interface. Also, only one page is not limited to only one file; we can have many templates in many different files.

Such applications can vary from a small simple **create**, **read**, **update**, and **delete** (**CRUD**), like a to-do list, until it reaches a more complex level with countless views, libraries, templates, scripts, and validations.

For a better example of a simple SPA, you can check out http://todomvc.com/; here, you can find a lot of information about many MVC frontend frameworks. The next paragraphs will show more about MVC on the client side.

The main goal about this kind of web application is to be able to update parts of an interface without sending or receiving a full-page request; this is perhaps the most interesting point about SPA.

SPA's popularity has been increasing in recent times, mainly because of its relative ease of development. This is because from the start, everything is done from the front-end of a web application using Ajax (to interacting with the server), HTML templates, a good MVC/MVVM framework, and of course, a lot of JavaScript.

Surely, we have a plethora of JavaScript frameworks that greatly facilitate our life as a developer, but how do we choose one from all these options? Which is the best option? What about the learning curve?

Throughout this chapter, we will understand the interaction models available between the most popular frameworks.

Before we begin our journey on SPAs, let's see the basic concept of the MVC/MVVM architecture.

Understanding the work of SPAs

What we see in this new world of web applications is an analogy to what had formerly been in software development on the server side, such as **Model View Controller** (**MVC**) or **Model View Presenter** (**MVP**). We will see **Model View ViewModel** (**MVVM**) in more detail in the next chapters.

Trygve Reenskaug introduced MVC into Smalltalk-76 while visiting Xerox Parc in the 1970s; In the 1980s, Jim Althoff et al implemented a version of MVC for the Smalltalk-80 class library. MVC was later expressed as a general concept in a 1988 article. More info can be found at `https://heim.ifi.uio.no/~trygver/themes/mvc/mvc-index.html`.

SPA has attracted a large number of developers lately, but what's so special or controversial in this development mode? What do these acronyms, MVC, MVP, and MVVM mean?

The answer to these questions is very simple; we can say this is all about JavaScript!

Wait a minute, JavaScript? You should be asking, "But what about HTML, CSS, server languages, and databases?" We'll understand it all and introduce what we call the full-stack developer using MEAN. However, we will take one step at a time.

Before we dive into the working of SPA, we need to learn about the MVC architecture.

Understanding the MVC/MVVM/MV* pattern

MVC is a software architecture pattern that emerged in the 1980s, and it separates the visual representation of information from the user's interaction.

However, we are talking about the MVC pattern on the client side, for example, JavaScript running on the client side, to be more specific, the web browser. Note that the majority of SPAs transfer to a web browser all the MVC logic used on the server with languages such as Java, C#, and Ruby.

We use JavaScript to model our application according to the standards of MVC on the client side and not on the server.

Another very important aspect is to understand what represents each development model, take a look at the following:

- **Presentation Model (PM)**
- **Model View Presenter (MVP)**
- **Model View Controller (MVC)**
- **Model View ViewModel (MVVM)**

Later in this chapter, we will see in more detail about these concepts. For now, let's take a look at the first appearance of MVVM.

In 2004, Martin Fowler published a small article about a design pattern called Presentation Model. The following is the pictorial representation of PM:

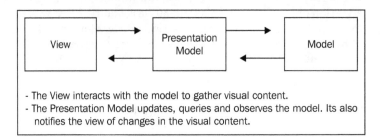

- The View interacts with the model to gather visual content.
- The Presentation Model updates, queries and observes the model. Its also notifies the view of changes in the visual content.

 You can see the original article here: `http://martinfowler.com/eaaDev/PresentationModel.html`

Approximately one year later, in 2005, John Gossman, a Microsoft architect for **Windows Presentation Foundation (WPF)** and Silverlight, revealed a new pattern on his blog, this time named as Model View ViewModel.

 John Gossman's original blog article can be found at `http://blogs.msdn.com/b/johngossman/archive/2005/10/08/478683.aspx`.

MVVM is very similar to Presentation Model; both patterns have an abstraction of a View (on the frontend, the view concept is what the client sees), which contains a View's state and behavior. The difference between them is that the MVVM model is more standardized and has been used in Silverlight for many years.

MVVM is based on MVC and MVP, which attempts to separate more clearly the development of **User Interfaces (UIs/**frontend) from that of the business logic and behavior in an application.

You might be asking, "but what does this have to do with SPA?"

 An awesome resource on the emergence of the MVVM model is available at `http://msdn.microsoft.com/en-us/magazine/dd419663.aspx`.

Nowadays, we can clearly see this type of implementation applied to some JavaScript frameworks such as Durandal.js, Kendo UI, Ember.js, AngularJS, and Knockout.js among others. Each of these has its own way to implement it; however, they have the same concept. The following is the pictorial representation of MVP:

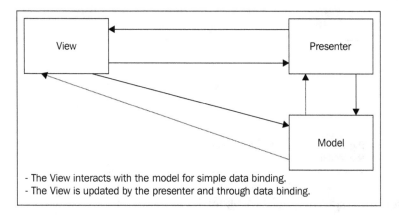

- The View interacts with the model for simple data binding.
- The View is updated by the presenter and through data binding.

 Backbone.js was the first MVC library to become popular, and it is an excellent alternative for the development of SPAs. For more information on it, check out http://backbonejs.org/.

Almost all the frameworks that we have today follows the standard MV* pattern. Now, let's review the concepts of MVVM:

- **Model**: This represents domain-specific data or information that our application will be working with. Models hold information, but typically don't handle behavior. They don't format information or influence how data appears in the browser as this isn't their responsibility.

- **View**: This is the only part of the application that the users actually interact with. It contains the data bindings and events and behaviors, it is an interactive UI that represents the state of a ViewModel. View isn't responsible for handling state—it keeps this in sync with ViewModel.

- **ViewModel**: This can be considered as a specialized Controller that acts as a data converter. It changes Model information into View information, passing commands from View to Model.

Views and ViewModels communicate using data-bindings and events. The following is the pictorial representation of how MVVM works:

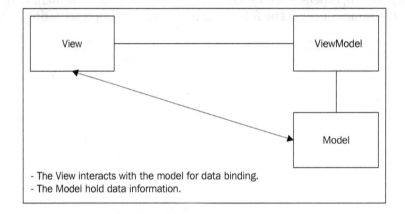

For a better understanding of MVVM, let's take a look at the two-way data binding, which is the core concept and one of the most important pieces in SPA. Due to data binding, we can update the interface with the changes made in the model and vice versa.

The concept of data binding is simplified as the process that establishes a connection between the application UI and business logic. It can also mean that when data is changed, the underlying data will reflect that change.

Let's see a more practical example in analogy to a JavaScript object.

Two-way data binding refers to the ability to bind changes to an object's properties to changes in the UI and vice versa. In other words, if we have a user object with the `name` property, whenever we assign a new value to `user.name`, the UI should show the new name. In the same way, if the UI includes an input field for the user's name, entering a value should cause the `name` property of the user object variable to be changed accordingly:

```
var user = {
  name : "fernando",
  age : 25
}
```

Both MVP and MVVM are derivatives of MVC. The key difference between both is the dependencies each layer has on the other layers, as well as how tightly bound they are with regard to each other.

In MVC, the **View** sits on top of our architecture with the **Controller** below it. **Models** sit below the controller, and so our Views know about our Controllers, and Controllers know about Models. Here, our Views have direct access to Models. However, exposing the complete Model to the View might have security and performance costs, depending on the complexity of our application. MVVM attempts to avoid these issues.

In MVP, the role of the controller is replaced with a **Presenter**. Presenters sit at the same level as views, listening to events from both **View** and **Model** and mediating the actions between them. Unlike MVVM, there isn't a mechanism to bind Views to ViewModels, so we instead rely on each View to implement an interface and allow Presenter to interact with View.

Pretty simple, right? However, we must be very careful in choosing the best tool for our work, or we can further complicate the performance of our application. The following screenshot shows an overview of the MVC, MVVM, and MVP I/O flow:

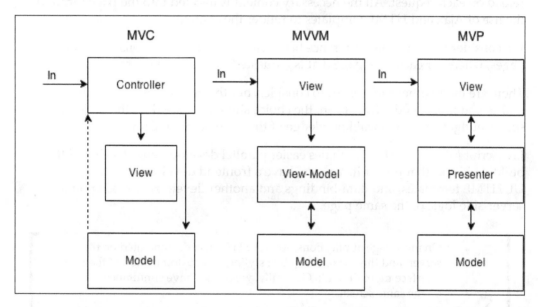

Of course, we have more names to care about such as Router, Collections, Events, and Sync but they are part of different implementations, as discussed in the book later.

There are numerous points to consider before building a new app; to make matters worse, the expansive web development landscape can be intimidating at the outset, but don't worry, we will detail everything.

Peculiarities between SPA and traditional web development

Let's now review some important points of employing the MVC/ MVVM pattern, to build web applications, instead of traditional web applications.

One of the important points is that the MVC pattern can be applied on the server side or client side. For example, we can use the MVC pattern that runs on the server using some JavaScript library as Express and build a SPA only on the server (in this case, Node.js). This is because MVC is a software architecture pattern and can be applied on both sides, frontend with MVC frontend frameworks and on server-side frameworks such as Ruby on Rails and .NET.

On SPA, everything happens on just one page; as mentioned before, there's no refresh on page request, such as in multipage applications where we have page reload on each request. All the necessary content is injected into the page through the use of Ajax and HTML templates to render the content.

We consider this the main difference between SPA and applications with multiple pages, where for each new page that is requested, we have a new request.

There are many other differences to consider, but the best tool is the one that makes you more productive. Then, the choice should be based on the project's scope, budget, and technical knowledge of the development team.

JavaScript MVVM or MV* facilitates easier parallel development of a UI and the building blocks that power it. You can have a frontend developer working on the UI, HTML templates, and data-bindings and another developer working on the server-side logic of the same page.

On multipage applications, we have HTML code generated on the server, and this makes the job of styling and customization of the user interface more difficult. Generally, we cannot have simultaneous work on the same screen.

Also, on multipage applications, the template used is the server-side template, so the web page is parsed and sent to the browser. However, in the case of SPA, the HTML code is generated on the fly according to the view, using some templates such as Handlebars and Underscores.

Choosing a library or framework

Frameworks generally have a greater number of methods and functions than just a small library, and furthermore its work might become more complex as the application grows.

We need to look at other important points as well:

- **The community behind the tool**: Often, there are active communities, and it is easy to find related stuff. However, obscure frameworks/libraries tend to have a small community behind them and a reduced number of online resources.

- **The frequency of updates**: Outdated frameworks/libraries have a larger number of errors, and the lack of frequent updates lead to more problems than you can possibly have.

- **Learning curve**: The higher the learning curve for a new tool, the greater the development time of your project. In a corporate environment, this can be very costly in the delivery of your project. A low learning curve lets you become more focused on building the application without having to worry about learning and solving problems at the same time.

- **Support to other libraries**: This lets you remove and add things without breaking your current code. Here, you can easily replace a library or code snippet for another without affecting the application.

- **Dependencies**: This shows how many dependent files you need to include in your project so that everything works and how all dependencies consume resources and transfer bandwidth. Successful applications tend to grow steadily, and consequently you will need to add some more dependencies.

- **Modularity**: Modular applications can be easily manipulated and can be scaled progressively. Modular systems have greater flexibility and reduce development costs. A framework that enables the use of modules is strongly recommended and not limited only to SPA but for all web applications.

Choosing a framework is the first and the most important choice you will make in the planning stage of the application. For sure, you'll want to choose the best framework or at least the most popular.

But how to choose? Every day we have new options emerging from simple libraries, and we also have small plugins to complex frameworks to choose from; so, how to decide?

Here, we make a simple list to ease your decision; you must keep in mind the following concepts about frameworks and libraries before you start:

- Libraries are snippets of codes, usually in the same file, and intended to solve a single problem. Often, they are fairly lightweight and have a very short learning curve.

- Frameworks are more robust and sometimes more heavy than simple libraries; they have a directory structure and a lot of concepts, conventions, and rules to follow. They have a long learning curve.

We can cite the following alternatives as libraries, where each of them propose to solve a specific problem or set of problems without the need for you to follow very rigid patterns of organizing code:

- Bootbox (simple alert messages)
- Knockout (data binds and observables)
- jQuery (DOM manipulation and effects)
- Rivets (data binding and templates)

The following are some frameworks; they all adopt a standard MVC/MVVM, as already mentioned:

- Ember
- Angular
- Kendo UI
- Backbone
- Meteor

Also, we need to mention some variations such as Durandal.js (Mixin jQuery, Knockout, Require.js), and Thorax.js (Mixin Backbone, Handlebars), which are widely used on the frontend, and others such as Express, Jade, and Handlebars (hbs) are used on the backend of the Node.js server.

 Handlebars is an incredible tool to build JavaScript templates on both the server and frontend; it is very lightweight and flexible and can be found at http://handlebarsjs.com/.

From the previous list, we can say that Kendo UI has all the peculiarities of MVVM frameworks with plus points such as UI components, data-bindings, and charts. Angular.js has the power to create your own directives and the most popularity with a huge community behind it.

So, what's best for your project? We need to answer some very important questions when choosing the right tool:

- How big is your project?
- Have you previously defined a structure or pattern?
- What kind of tasks you need to solve and are they simple?
- How short are the deadlines? Will you have time to learn a very complex framework?

These are the questions you should answer first. After this, when you're choosing, take into account how many applications are already in production that use your choice.

Trello, Foursquare, Code School, DocumentCloud, and Groupon are good examples of using some of the mentioned frameworks in real applications.

We believe that all tools have good and bad sides, the pros and cons, but we also believe that the best tool is one which best solves our problem. Thus, be careful when choosing the tool and analyze the mentioned facts well; some of them can make you save your time and money.

A very practical example is the need for nested views in templates; a precipitous choice cannot pay attention to this detail, and you will certainly have a lot of work if the chosen tool is not present in a similar default solution for nested views.

Now, for instance, you know how to use a particular library and try to integrate it with another and discover that there is no compatibility between them. In such cases, you will need more time to try to resolve this impediment.

Introducing the MEAN stack

Before we proceed, we need to know more about the MEAN concept.

MEAN stands for:

- MongoDB, the database
- Express, the server-side web framework
- AngularJS, the frontend framework
- Node.js, the server

Node.js has the ability to run JavaScript on the server and use the power of the Express framework to build an HTTP proxy and routes.

MongoDB is an open source database document oriented for high performance and scalability and is also known as NoSQL database.

 All you need to know about Express can be found at `http://expressjs.com/`.
To know more about MongoDB, check out `http://www.mongodb.org/`.

The Node.js community is growing each day and the stack will fast become more and more stable, and with the number of Node and Express boilerplates growing, we have good options in our hands.

Thus, we can consider MEAN as a great way for the development of SPAs.

The opinions are certainly much divided when it comes to SPA, but SPA is about dealing with a lot of frontend development.

Of course, we can use any kind of server-side technology such as .Net, PHP, Python, and Ruby on Rails.

Most likely, the solutions and examples presented in the next chapters are not intended to be the final word nor establish new standards or criticize any form of development that exists.

The solutions found here were adapted to our sample application and the book proposal to show some ways to develop SPAs.

Tools to develop web applications

Today, we have a variety of tools to help us in developing web applications. The correct choice of the best tool can save time and money.

We will now see some indispensable tools and editors for agile frontend development of SPAs. All the following tools mentioned are open source, except the Visual Studio and WebStorm IDEs. Here, we list the characteristics that we use in our sample project, with AngularJS and Node.js.

Text editor

You can choose the editor of your choice; however, we recommend two of the most used editors in our community.

One is called WebStorm and provides a complete development environment; you can download the trial version at http://www.jetbrains.com/webstorm/. Webstorm has built-in tools, such as Terminal, RESTClient, Grunt.js support and **Node Package Manager** (**NPM**); they are at your fingertips for efficient development.

It also supports syntax highlight for languages such as HTML5, Node.js, Typescript, CoffeeScript, Dart, EJS, Handlebars, Mustache, Web Components, Stylus, Less, Sass, Jade, and JSLint/JSHint.

Until Version 7, it was possible to use an AngularJS plugin to facilitate the work. The plugin provides a number of advantages such as autocomplete, easy navigation between your modules, controllers, and directives.

The AngularJS plugin is very simple to use; just perform the following steps:

1. Navigate to **File** | **Settings** | **Plugins**.
2. Click on **Browse Repositories**.
3. Select **AngularJS**.
4. Double-click (or right-click) and when prompted, choose **Yes**.
5. Restart WebStorm.

Remember that the preceding procedure applies to all versions until 8.0.2. From Version 8.0.4 the support is bundled with WebStorm. And to start using, you just need to include the AngularJS library in your project.

The other widely used text editor is Sublime Text; it is a very popular and powerful editor because it is lightweight and supports many languages. You can download it for free from http://www.sublimetext.com/2.

The Sublime Text editor has a great plugin to work with AngularJS, which is very similar to Webstorm.

You can find more information about the plugin at https://github.com/angular-ui/AngularJS-sublime-package/archive/master.zip.

Also, it can be installed directly from Sublime Package Control.

It provides autocompletion of core AngularJS directives, such as `ng-repeat`, `ng-click`, as well as any custom directives you create.

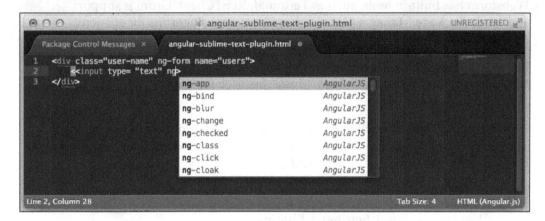

 You must have the Package Control plugin installed so as to be able to install any other plugins. You can find more details about Package Control at `http://wbond.net/sublime_packages/ package_control`.

AngularJS

AngularJS is a client-side framework for MVC/MVVM done in JavaScript. The standard adopted is the closest to the MVVM pattern and is very robust and highly suitable for SPA. Later, we will discuss more thoroughly the basic features that we will use on the sample application.

You can find the whole documentation about AngularJS at `http://docs.angularjs.org/tutorial`.

AngularJS lets you write client-side web applications as if you have a smarter browser. It lets you use good old HTML (or Haml, Jade, and others) as your template language and lets you extend HTML's syntax to express your application's components clearly and succinctly. It automatically synchronizes data from your UI (view) with your JavaScript objects (model) through two-way data binding. Furthermore, it is possible to extend it by creating directives and customized elements.

Debugging tools

We also have an important tool to debug SPAs built with AngularJS, the Chrome extension called Angular Batarang, and it can be found for free at `https://github.com/angular/angularjs-batarang`.

Batarang provides us with a Chrome-like Web Inspector. After installing, you can activate it by pressing *F12* or clicking the right mouse button on the screen and selecting the last link, **Inspect element**.

The Batarang extension has five tabs: **Model**, **Performance**, **Dependencies**, **Options**, and **Help**, thus providing a complete environment to debug your application.

The following is a screenshot of the Batarang panel:

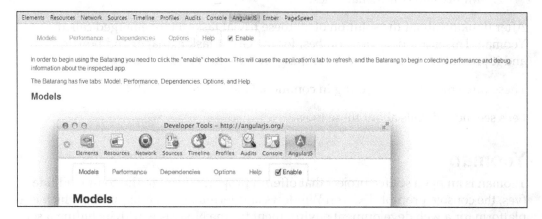

There is an alternative to the Firefox browser known as AngScope. It is very useful to inspect `$scope` in your AngularJS project.

You can find it through the add-ons for Firefox or download it from `https://addons.mozilla.org/pt-BR/firefox/addon/angscope-simple-angularjs-s/`.

Generators and the task manager

Nowadays, to start developing a web application is a very laborious task. For this, a lot of settings are required, a well-defined directories structure, some frameworks and boilerplates, a compiler for preprocessors, such as Less, Sass, CoffeScript, among other things.

You can lose a lot of time in the initial configurations of the project. You'll certainly need to repeat it all with every new project.

The following are some common steps to every new application:

1. Scaffolding folders.
2. Download some libraries.
3. Download some template engines.
4. Download some frameworks.
5. Configure a testing environment.
6. Create a local web server to serve the contents during development.
7. Minify and concatenate files.

After thinking about the solution of all these trivial tasks a tool emerged called Yeoman. This is a code generator, besides the Grunt task manager and Bower, and it promotes a new way of developing web applications.

These three tools have one thing in common: Node.js and the NPM.

Let's see more details about these tools.

Yeoman

Yeoman is an open source project that offers a program through the command line (yes, the console prompt/DOS on Windows and terminal on Linux/OSX), which is a platform for a web development environment for the Node.js world, including a set of libraries and generators.

In addition, there is a plethora of web generators for the main frameworks in the market such as Angular, Ember, and Backbone. It has an official repository that can be found at `http://yeoman.io/generators/official.html`, plus a repository of generators provided by the community too.

Yeoman is a tool that suggests an established workflow and can be incorporated into your projects. The installation is pretty simple, just open your terminal window and type the following command:

```
npm install -g yo
```

 You need to have Node.js installed on your machine. Grunt and Bower will also be installed.

Bower

Bower is a manager dependency for the Web, but specifically for frontend packages. The idea is simple: you list the dependencies of the JavaScript example (AnglularJS, Pure CSS, Responsive boilerplate) in a file called `bower.json` at the root of your project, and with this, you can control the installation/upgrade of these packages through the command line.

Installing Bower globally on your system is very simple; just type the following command:

```
npm install -g bower
```

Do not forget to use the `sudo` command if you are not the system administrator and are using Linux or Mac OS X.

You can find more information about Bower at `http://bower.io/`

If you have already installed Yeoman, you don't need to install Bower or Grunt.

Another configuration setup is the `.bowerrc` file placed in the root directory. Here, we can set up the folder name and destiny to the Bower packages:

```
{
    "directory": "public/lib"
}
```

If you don't do this, Bower will install the dependencies in the `bower_components` folder, in the root project by default.

Grunt

Grunt is a tool to automate build tasks done entirely in JavaScript. If you are following the best practices for performance, then you should worry about minifying CSS and JavaScript files to reduce the number of requests. You can also use a preprocessor to generate your CSS, like Less and Sass, or even make some CSS Sprites for your images.

A validation tool such as JSLint verifies errors on JavaScript files, CSSLint for consistence in CSS and many others actions, as mentioned before.

Using all this individually is insane if you want to automate this whole process. This is why Grunt.js is very useful and mandatory to any web project.

To install Grunt on your machine, just type the following command in your terminal window:

```
npm install grunt-cli
```

While these three tools represent the necessary triad for a fast web development environment, it is not obligatory. All tools can be installed one at a time as explained, or in general using Yeoman.

The SPA directory structure

There's lots of consensus among the main frameworks and libraries about how to do MVC architecture, declarative bindings, and so on. Your choice will deeply influence your architecture.

Some frameworks recommend a specific directory structure to be followed, but some others are more flexible.

We'll adopt a boilerplate to build our API in the next chapters, and we'll discuss more about server structure and code organization; we should always think with regard to maintenance and scalability of the application. For now, let's see an example of a basic structure in detail that is very common to all MVC patterns:

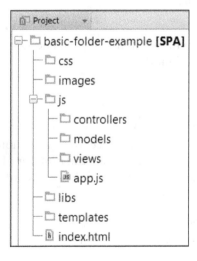

A simple basic SPA folder structure consists of the following:

- **Basic-folder-example [SPA]**: This folder is the root of our application and has our one main file, **index.html**.
- **CSS**: This folder contains all stylesheets.
- **images**: This folder contains all images.
- **js**: This has all the subfolders and a file called **app.js** (our startup file).
- **controllers** folder: This contains all controllers' files, but we can name this as Collections or ViewModels depending on what kind of library or framework we will be using.
- **models**: This folder contains all model files.
- **views**: This folder has all view files (only data, no HTML rendering here).
- **libs**: This contains all third-party libraries such as jQuery, Handlebars, and Knockout.
- **templates**: This folder has all script templates such as Handlebars, Underscore. Note that this folder contains all the templates we will use in our application.

Note that we don't have any folder to deal with routes, but from a basic application, we can put our routing logic in our app.js or server.js file.

 In Node.js applications, often the initialization file is called app.js or server.js and is always in the root directory of the application.

Despite being a very basic structure, it is sufficient for understanding the basics of folder names. Of course, as things are getting complex, we need to re-evaluate this structure (maybe include a folder for Sass or Less files and also add some other things). However, in the course of the book, we will see some alternatives.

It's all about JavaScript

As mentioned before, all SPAs are made with JavaScript, and of course, where you have a lot of JavaScript you can easily get in trouble if you don't take notice of code organization.

We recommend that you use some validation tools such as JSLINT and JSHINT and also a validation tool for JSON files such as JSONLint. The following are the links for these validation tools:

- JSLint: `http://www.jslint.com/`
- JSHint: `http://www.jshint.com/`
- JSONLint: `http://jsonlint.com/`

The main difference between LINT and HINT is that LINT validates indentation and HINT doesn't.

HTML, CSS, and the responsive way

Now that we have seen a general overview about the tools to ease our life in MVVM/MV client-side development, we take a look at two tools that will help us on the interface with HTML and CSS.

As the goal of the book is not to be the absolute guide for interface design, we introduce here a simple library build with only HTML and CSS as its name makes clear, Pure CSS.

Pure CSS

This tool provides us with a complete user interface with several components for forms, tables, menus, buttons, and everything else we need to build robust interfaces. The main point here, is the ability to build the interface components without JavaScript behaviors and can be downloaded for free from `http://purecss.io/`.

Pure is ridiculously tiny. The entire set of modules adds up to 4.5 KB when minified and zipped. Crafted with mobile devices in mind, it is important to us to keep our file sizes small, and every line of CSS was carefully considered (source: `http://purecss.io/`).

The important point here is that despite being directed to complete and responsive design, we can use it in a modular way and not have to depend on your responsive grid system, which although very useful in applications is not necessary for our examples.

With this in mind, we chose another responsive grid system called Responsive boilerplate; it is very simple to use with only three main classes and twelve columns. It can also be downloaded for free from `http://www.responsiveboilerplate.com`.

Responsive boilerplate is a lightweight (1.5 KB) cross-browser grid system, elegant and minimalist, made with only three main classes and 12 columns. It is built with mobile first in mind, fits any screen size, and is prepacked with some extra CSS helpers for mobile devices.

It also has a series of snippets for the Sublime Text editor, which can be downloaded from `https://github.com/newaeonweb/ResponsiveBoilerplateSnippets`.

It can also be simply installed via Package Control on Sublime Text. The package is very complete and makes our development process very fast, as we can see in the following screenshot:

Also, we can install both Pure CSS and Responsive Boilerplate with Bower. It's very simple; just type the following commands in terminal:

```
bower install responsiveboilerplate
bower install purecss
```

We will cover this in practice in the upcoming chapters.

There is also a series of templates to develop SPAs provided by the community behind the Microsoft for IDE Visual Studio 2012, which can be downloaded for free from `http://www.asp.net/single-page-application/overview/templates`.

> All the tools mentioned in this chapter are open source and maintained by the community development, except the Visual Studio and WebStorm IDEs.
>
> You should choose tools that are useful and productive for your development environment.

Summary

As we have seen, the development of applications of Single Page can be extremely complex and have countless resources at our disposal, from simple text editors to IDEs such as WebStorm and Visual Studio.

What happens in almost every SPA is that the data traffic from the database to the User interface is done through a common restful API using the JSON file format.

The next chapter will dive deep into RESTful applications with the MongoDB and Express frameworks running a Node.js server. We will also check the main concepts of Node, such as the event loop and callbacks.

2
Taking a Deep Dive into Node.js and MongoDB

A built-in asynchronous I/O, single-threaded or even multithreaded, real-time applications, sockets, and HTTP connections make Node.js the most powerful tool to create web servers that run JavaScript on the server side.

MongoDB is agile, scalable, document-oriented schema less, and high performance, which makes it one of the most popular NoSQL databases. Node.js and MongoDB unleashed all the power for high-performance web applications with Express, a lightweight web framework that supports template engines, routing, and flash notices. It's very similar to Sinatra from Ruby. Moving forward, we will see some of the key concepts about all of these tools.

The following will be covered in the chapter:

- Node server, NPM, and middlewares
- Event-driven development and the event loop
- Working with `require()` and modules
- Express, a web framework on a server
- MongoDB and the terminal
- The MongoDB connection with Mongoose
- Mongoose schemas and models

Node server, NPM, and middleware

Node is a web server built with JavaScript and the basic Node.js proposal is of high performance and scalable web applications, but what does it really mean?

In other server-side programming languages, such as Java, PHP, and .NET, each connection starts a new thread on the server potentially, and in general is accompanied by 2 MB of memory. On a server that has 8 GB of RAM, this defines the maximum number of concurrent connections as about 4,000 users. Now, imagine that your application is growing and every day gets more and more hits; you probably will need more servers or even to invest in more hardware. This is the bottleneck of the whole architecture of web applications, the maximum number of concurrent I/O connections a server can handle and keep stable. Node.js solves this by changing how a connection is made to the server. Instead of starting a new thread for each connection, it creates a process that does not require a memory block to accompany it. It does not block outgoing calls directly to I/O.

Node servers can support tens of thousands of simultaneous connections. It does not allocate one thread per connection model, but uses a model process per connection, creating only the memory that is required for each connection. It achieves its goals by providing highly scalable servers.

Actually, Node changes the panorama of the server and the bottleneck of the whole system from the maximum number of connections to the maximum traffic capacity of the system. It also features a powerful package manager called **NPM** (**Node Package Manager**); though it is possible to install and update packages, you can still create your own packages and publish them online for the whole community. It is also worth noting that many third-party tools, such as Grunt, Bower, and Yeoman among others, use Node to install packages.

NPM is a command-line utility that interacts with an online open source repository of projects for Node.js; it is possible to install modules and manage dependencies and versions.

The NPM repository already has more than 76,000 packages, all of which are open source libraries, and many are added every day. These applications can be found through the search portal of NPM. You can search and discover a lot of packages at the official repository at `https://www.npmjs.org/`. You can found out more about Node.js at `http://nodejs.org/`.

Another important use of NPM is the ability to install its own modules and dependencies. When you have a Node project with a file named `package.json`, you can run the `npm install` command in the root folder of your project and NPM will install all dependencies listed in `package.json`.

In addition, the NPM `init` command starts the configuration of your project through a step-by-step configuration to create a `package.json` file from scratch.

The most used commands are:

- `npm install module_name`: This installs a module in the project
- `npm install module_name-save`: This installs the module and adds it to the list of dependencies on `package.json`
- `npm list`: This lists all modules in the project
- `npm list-g`: This lists all global modules
- `npm remove module_name`: This uninstalls a module
- `module_name npm update`: This updates the module version
- `npm -v`: This displays the current version of NPM
- `npm adduser username`: This creates a user on the NPM repository
- `npm whoami`: This displays details of your public profile on the NPM repository
- `npm publish`: This publishes your module on the NPM repository

Another key part of Node is called middleware. We often define middleware as bridges between snippet codes where all the flow passes through them. On a Node environment, this is very common. We have a lot of Middleware such as `connect`, `body-parser` (very useful to work with JSON), `cookie parser`, and many more. These are part of the Express (v4) web framework as separate modules, and we will see more about them later in the book.

Event-driven development and the event loop

Event-driven development came from event-driven programming, in other words, outside the paradigm of object-oriented programming, event-based programming is the ability to treat the application flow after an event is fired.

JavaScript is a great language for event-driven programming; it allows anonymous functions and closures, and more importantly, the syntax is very familiar with other programming languages. The callback functions that are called when an event occurs can be written in the same place where you capture the event. Therefore, it is easy to code and easy to maintain your application.

Almost everything in Node uses callbacks. Node callbacks are functions that will be implemented in the asynchronous mode. In general, a callback function is one that is passed as an argument to another function using function pointers. For example, it tells a function to perform some task and when finished with this task, perform another task.

The event loop

Another important point to mastering Node.js is the event loop. Any developer familiar with jQuery used to handle callbacks functions, usually triggered after the user performs some task, such as a click on an accordion component or a slideshow or even a simple button. However, in Node.js, the event loop starts when an application starts. Functions have callbacks to other functions and the event loop only ends when the last callback is performed, as shown in the following figure:

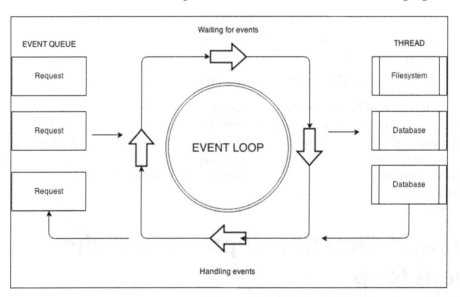

The event loop is always there and keeps checking whether the functions are explicitly finished; otherwise it keeps the program going and the actions asynchronous. Let's take a look at a very simple and common example to create a HTTP server:

```
var http = require('http');
http.createServer(function (req, res) {
    res.writeHead(200, {'Content-Type': 'text/plain'});
    res.end('Hello World\n');
}).listen(3000, "127.0.0.1");
console.log('Server running at http://127.0.0.1:3000/');
```

Note that our HTTP server attaches a callback to the `request` event. The callback is passed to `createServer` as an argument.

Node.js runs the code from top to bottom; as we attached some event listeners, Node.js doesn't exit, but waits for an event to be fired. When an HTTP request is sent to the server, Node.js goes to the `request` event that generates the callbacks attached to this event so as to be run in order.

In the preceding example, we have only one callback, which is the anonymous function we passed as an argument to `createServer`. However, in a real application, we can have many functions.

Working with require() and modules

Node.js follows CommonJS, a specification for the JavaScript ecosystem. The inline function, `require()`, is the easiest way to include existing modules in separate files.

The require() function

The basic behavior of `require()` is that it reads the JavaScript file, interprets the script, and then returns the content of the `exports` object. The following code is a sample module to understand it better; copy the code, paste in a new file, and save this file as `example.js`:

```
console.log("Running through the example");

var requireExample = function () {
  console.log("requireExample");
}

exports.greetings = "Hello Node";

exports.sayHi = function () {
  console.log(exports.greetings);
}
```

We can test our module that runs through the node REPL (the Node console). Open terminal if you are on Mac/Linux or Command Prompt if you are on Windows, go to the code folder, and start the Node console. Here, simply type `node` without passing any file as a parameter and it will open in the REPL mode. Then, just type `require("./example.js")` to import our module. We have the following output:

```
> require("./example.js")
Running through the example
{ greetings: 'Hello Node',
  sayHi: [Function] }
```

Here, you can see that the module has been imported successfully, and it was stated that the function requires the script to be played first. It then prints `Running through the example` in the first row and returns the contents of the `exports` object, which contains only two objects, `greetings: 'Hello Node'` and `sayHi: [Function]`. The invisible function was not imported because it was not assigned to the `exports` object.

> **Read-Eval-Print Loop (REPL)** is a simple and interactive program that first reads phrases or sections of a program, then evaluates (or runs) it, and finally prints the result.

However, if we want to use the function to `sayHi` of our module, we see that it is not available in the global context and the error message will tell you that `sayHi` is not defined.

To be able to use the functions imported from a module, we have to import it and assign the `return` function to a `require` variable. In the code, if we run `test = require ('. / example.js')` on REPL, our `example.js` script will be evaluated and the object instance will receive {`greetings: 'Hello Node'`, `sayHi: [Function]` }, which is the `return` function. In this manner, you can easily access the `sayHi` function, as shown in the following code:

```
>  test = require ("./example.js")
{ greetings: 'Hello Node',
   sayHi: [Function] }
> test.sayHi()
Hello Node
undefined
```

Now, let's see how to use `module.exports` to assign a function or a new object for `exports`; copy the following code and save as `example-module.js` at the same place where the `example.js` file was saved:

```
module.exports = function () {
   console.log("Hello Node from module.exports")
}
```

Open the REPL and type:

```
require('./example-module.js')()
```

This time, when importing the module with `require`, it first interprets (evaluates and performs) the code, which causes the module to import and call itself.

At the end, `require` returns the function attributed to `exports`, generating the following output:

```
> require('./example-module.js')
Hello Node from module.exports
[Function]
```

The last line, `[Function]`, confirms that the return value of `require ('. / example-module.js')` is a function and the `Hello from Node module.exports` message confirms that the code was interpreted before being returned to this function. It is important to say that the code is interpreted only the first time it is imported; if you import it more than once, then the `require` function will re-export the object that is already saved in cache.

Another important thing to have in mind is about the way `require` fetches the files. If the file starts with `. /`, then it is considered a relative path to the file that called `require`. If the file starts with `/`, then it is considered to belong to the absolute address. The file extension is not necessary; you can just declare a dependency like this: `var express = require ('express');`. Node.js interprets this as `express.js`.

If the filename passed to `require` is the name of a directory, the function will first search in a file called `package.json` in the directory and then load the file referenced in the `main` property. Otherwise, the function will look for a file called `index.js` inside the `module` folder.

The Node modules

Node has a simple module loading system. The use of modules allows you to include other JavaScript files in your application, as we saw when we used `require()`. Modules are very important for building applications on Node because they allow you to include external libraries, such as libraries for database access, libraries for authentication, and so on, and also help to organize the code into separate parts with limited responsibilities.

Downloading the example code

You can download the example code files from your account at `http://www.packtpub.com`for all the Packt Publishing books you have purchased. If you purchased this book elsewhere, you can visit `http://www.packtpub.com/support` and register to have the files e-mailed directly to you.

Also you can check the book repository on GitHub at: `https://github.com/newaeonweb/conference-api`

One of the simplest solutions for JavaScript modules adopted as standard by Node is the CommonJS standard with minor differences. CommonJS offers first-class modules, which in turn have the same importance of first-class functions. It says that something is a first-class object in a programming language when it can be built at runtime, passed as a parameter, assigned to a variable, or returned as the result of a function. Importantly, `exports` is a reference to `module.exports` used only to add objects. If you want to export a single item, such as a `constructor`, you will need to use the `module.exports` object directly. Let's take a look at an example of how to use it:

```
// myConstructor.js example
function MyConstructor ( ) {

}

// On Node REPL
module.exports = MyConstructor;
```

In each module is a `module` variable referenced to the object that represents the current module. In particular, `module.exports` is accessible via a global `exports` module. The object module is not actually global, but a local object of each module.

The `module.exports` object is created by the system and Node modules export variable points to this object. Your module might return multiple objects and functions by simply adding them to the `export` variable, for example, `exports.sayHi = function () {console.log ('Hello Node')}`.

Another key concept of the Node module is a set of default variables available in the scope of each module; the following are the most common variables:

- `__filename`: This is the filename of the code being executed.
- `__dirname`: This is the name of the directory in which you saved the script that is being executed.
- `process`: This is an object that is associated with the process that is currently running. In addition to variables, this object has methods such as `process.exit`, `process.cwd`, and `process.uptime`.
- `process.argv`: This is an array that contains the command-line arguments. The first element is the node, the second element is the name of the JavaScript file, and the next will be all the arguments of an additional command line if they are assigned.
- `process.stdin`, `process.stout`, and `process.stderr`: These streams correspond to the standard input, standard output, and standard error output of the current process.

- `process.env`: This is an object that contains the user environment variables of the current process.
- `require.main`: When a file is executed by Node directly, `require.main` is assigned to this module.

Much more should be written about all the Node particularities, but this is beyond the main scope of our book; what we present here is the basis for our understanding.

Express – a web framework on a server

Express is the most common and flexible framework to build web applications on Node. It provides us with a robust set of features to deal with such as SPA, the RESTful API, and of course, the MEAN stack. The Express framework has full support for templates and rendering using the Jade engine as the default. It is very suitable for large-scale applications that render HTML on the server side.

Of course, we have others options such as the amazing restify microframework, strictly built to deal with the RESTful API, but as we are talking about MEAN, we use only the acronym-related technology, which is Express.

Jade is a template engine uniquely for Node, inspired by Ruby and Haml with rule-based indentation, like the Sass and Python syntax. More information on Jade can be found at `http://jade-lang.com/`.

The main reason to use Express is that the default Node API is not as robust for complex applications, as every route management and other features are treated in a very basic way. Express follows good development practices, an oriented RESTful architecture that uses the main methods of the HTTP protocol (such as GET, POST, PUT, and DELETE), and very difficult-to-build complex web applications.

We can list some great features of Express:

- Powerful routing management
- Redirect for helpers
- Can use any view template engine
- Prepared to use RESTful
- Application mounting
- High performance
- Views rendering
- Partials support

It is important to talk about the template engine as the Express framework uses Jade by default and has its own syntax, but it is possible to use others engines such as **Embedded JavaScript (EJS)** that renders HTML directly.

As our scope is directed at building SPA and the tools that we'll use in our frontend already have their own syntax for templates, we will not go deeper into templates that run on the server.

It is important to say that Express is also the basis for the creation of other frameworks for Node such as Locomotive, Kraken, and many others. To have a brief idea of the ease of use of the Express framework, note how simple it is to create an application, as shown in the following code:

```
var express = require('express');
var app = express();

app.get('/', function(req, res){
  res.send('Hello Express');
});

app.listen(3000);
```

Certainly, an application will contain many lines of code, but here, it is possible to see how easy it is to create an application using Express. Just with a few lines of code, we can generate a message with `Hello Express` running on a Node server.

MongoDB and the terminal

MongoDB, also known as NoSQL database, is a document-oriented database; this means that all the data is stored like a JSON file.

Instead of storing your data in tables and rows as you would do with a relational database, MongoDB stores this data in the key-value format, using **binary JSON (BSON)**; developers can easily map to modern object-oriented languages, without a complicated ORM layer. This new data model simplifies coding significantly and also improves the performance of the grouping of the relevant data together internally.

MongoDB is not limited to a two-dimensional approach to a relational database where we have rows and columns; it can represent objects in the real world as complex and unique as they are. Imagine that in your relational database, you must enter a new attribute to a record; for this, your changes in this model should be applied to the entire database.

Comparing a relational database with the NoSQL database

In the case of MongoDB, you can apply them only where it is necessary and not in all cases, as in the relational model, where normally it creates a new column in the related table, as we can see in the following screenshot:

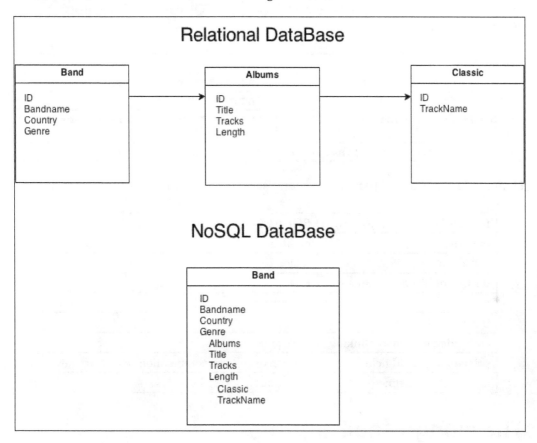

The basic idea here is that a document should be self-contained with all the information in the same place. Why is this? Simply, because instead of performing a query with multiple joins such as the relational model, MongoDB executes a single query, which returns the entire document. The result is more performance. MongoDB is a document-based NoSQL database without transactions and joins.

Another important fact about relational databases is that they require that schemas be defined before inserting data; in MongoDB, you don't need a predefined schema to insert the data.

You can find more about the advantages of NoSQL at `http://www.mongodb.com/nosql-explained`.

For a better understanding, let's take a look at some SQL commands against MongoDB commands.

MongoDB	SQL
`db.name.insert({ A:1, B:2 })`	`INSERT INTO NAME VALUES(A, B)`
`db.users.find()`	`SELECT * FROM users`
`db.bands.find({ name: "Metallica" })`	`SELECT * FROM bands WHERE name = "Metallica"`
`db.bands.find().limit(5).skip(10)`	`SELECT * FROM bands LIMIT 5 SKIP 10`

Here's a table to exemplify more differences:

MongoDB terminology	SQL terminology
database	database
collection	table
document/BSON document	row
field	column
index	index
embedded document/linking	table joins
primary key is _id field	column or column combination as primary key
aggregation pipeline	aggregation: group by

The mongo shell

Now that we have a brief idea of the power and simplicity of MongoDB, let's learn how to interact using the terminal. This book assumes that you already have MongoDB installed on your machine. Go straight to the terminal and type `mongo`.

Once you start the MongoDB shell, you will come across a message similar to this:

```
MongoDB shell version: 2.4.6
connecting to: test
> _
```

As we haven't specified any database yet, note that the shell starts in a MongoDB database called test. You can use it for these basic examples; however, we will create a new database using the following steps so that we can get some familiarity with MongoDB shell commands:

1. Type use exampledb in the terminal, and you will get the following message:

    ```
    > use exampledb
    switched to db exampledb
    > _
    ```

    This message indicates that MongoDB created and switched to the new database named exampledb. Note that no extra command was used beyond the keyword uses to create the new database, so only one command is necessary to create and switch from test to exampledb.

2. Now, we can create our collections easily using the simple JSON format with the insert command:

    ```
    db.bands.insert({
        name: "Metallica",
        album: "Master of Puppets",
        tracks: 9,
        year: "1996"
    })
    ```

    All commands in MongoDB are extremely simple and very easy to memorize; moreover, when any questions arise, we have the help() command, where we can perform our search quickly.

3. We can apply this on databases and collections, for example, db.collection-name.help().

The following screenshot illustrates the output when we apply the `help()` command to the speakers collection:

```
db.speakerdb.find(...).count()
db.speakerdb.find(...).limit(n)
db.speakerdb.find(...).skip(n)
db.speakerdb.find(...).sort(...)
db.speakerdb.findOne([query])
db.speakerdb.findAndModify( { update : ... , remove : bool [, query: {}, sort: {}, 'new': false] } )
db.speakerdb.getDB() get DB object associated with collection
db.speakerdb.getPlanCache() get query plan cache associated with collection
db.speakerdb.getIndexes()
db.speakerdb.group( { key : ..., initial: ..., reduce : ...[, cond: ...] } )
db.speakerdb.insert(obj)
db.speakerdb.mapReduce( mapFunction , reduceFunction , <optional params> )
db.speakerdb.aggregate( [pipeline], <optional params> ) - performs an aggregation on a collection; returns a cursor
db.speakerdb.remove(query)
db.speakerdb.renameCollection( newName , <dropTarget> ) renames the collection.
db.speakerdb.runCommand( name , <options> ) runs a db command with the given name where the first param is the collection name
db.speakerdb.save(obj)
db.speakerdb.stats()
db.speakerdb.storageSize() - includes free space allocated to this collection
db.speakerdb.totalIndexSize() - size in bytes of all the indexes
db.speakerdb.totalSize() - storage allocated for all data and indexes
db.speakerdb.update(query, object[, upsert_bool, multi_bool]) - instead of two flags, you can pass an object with fields: upsert, multi
db.speakerdb.validate( <full> ) - SLOW
db.speakerdb.getShardVersion() - only for use with sharding
db.speakerdb.getShardDistribution() - prints statistics about data distribution in the cluster
db.speakerdb.getSplitKeysForChunks( <maxChunkSize> ) - calculates split points over all chunks and returns splitter function
db.speakerdb.getWriteConcern() - returns the write concern used for any operations on this collection, inherited from server/db if set
db.speakerdb.setWriteConcern( <write concern doc> ) - sets the write concern for writes to the collection
db.speakerdb.unsetWriteConcern( <write concern doc> ) - unsets the write concern for writes to the collection
```

Don't worry about what is inside the speakers collection; later in the book, we'll create the collection together.

Besides the shell that comes by default with the installation of MongoDB, we have some third-party software facilitators that assist us with the graphical interface rather than the administration of our databases in MongoDB. A good option is UMongo and you can download it for free at `http://www.edgytech.com/umongo/`; they have different versions for Windows, Linux, and Mac OS X. It is very similar to SQL Manager and can help us a lot in getting a full view of all our databases.

 More administrative interface tools can be found at `http://docs.mongodb.org/ecosystem/tools/administration-interfaces/`.

As we are talking about a database, a common question is how to connect the database with our application?

In the Node ecosystem, everything is planned. We have many options in hand to deal with all kind of projects, as we will see in another powerful tool to handle connections and schemes.

MongoDB connection with Mongoose

Mongoose is a Node library solution that provides a schema-based model to the data of our application. It has type conversion, validation, creating queries, and business logic hooks to system, and thanks to MongoDB, it also has a flexible schema.

Mongoose provides a mapping of objects similar to MongoDB **Object Relational Mapping** (ORM) or **Object Data Mapping** (ODM) in the case of Mongoose. This means that Mongoose translates data from the database to JavaScript objects that can be used by our application. It was born to work in an asynchronous environment.

Furthermore, as we saw earlier, we can install it easily using NPM with the simple command: `npm install mongoose`. Mongoose will be available to the entire application; you just need add it to the application file, as shown in the following example:

```
var mongoose = require('mongoose'); mongoose.connect('mongodb://
localhost/test');

var db = mongoose.connection;

db.on('error', console.error.bind(console, 'connection error:'));
db.once('open', function callback () { // Hello Mongoose });
```

Note that our string connection points to `http://localhost/databasename` and the name after the slash is our database name. In a real-world application or on a production environment, we need to pass the username and password for the database user.

Mongoose schemas and models

All we need is a schema and a model for us to work with the data to be persisted on our MongoDB database. Schemas define the structure of documents within a collection and models are used to create instances of data to be stored in documents.

The schema types are:

- String
- Number
- Date
- Buffer
- Boolean
- Mixed
- ObjectId
- Array

When thinking about it, we imagine how we can represent our collection of bands from the previous example using models and schema. The following code shows bandSchema and the Band model:

```
var bandSchema = new Mongoose.Schema({
  name:  { type: String },
  album: { type: String },
  track: { type: Number },
  year:  { type: Number }
});


var Band = Mongoose.model('Band', bandSchema);
```

The last line of the code compiles the Band model using bandSchema as the structure. Mongoose also creates a collection called Band for these documents. You might notice that the Band model is capitalized, as when a model is compiled, it returns a constructor function that will be used to create one or more instances of the model.

This model's instances are the documents that will be persisted by MongoDB using the save function. So, to create a new document, Band can be used, as it is easier now that we have defined the model. We just instantiate the Band model and save this instance on the database, as shown in the following code:

```
var slayer = new Band({
  name: "Slayer",
  album: Show no Mercy,
  track: "10",
  year: 1984
});


slayer.save(function(err) {
  if (err) return console.error(err);
  console.dir(slayer);
});
```

Note that we use a string instead of a number in the track property. Mongoose will be responsible for converting the data type specified in bandSchema.

When we add these two code to the database and execute our application, we see that the `save` function will provide a newly created document; look at the console:

```
{ __v: 0,
  name: 'Slayer',
  album: 'Show no Mercy',
  track: 10,
  year: 1984,
  _id: 8334012cb65dfgf003000002 }
```

Collections in MongoDB have a flexible schema; this means that collections do not impose the structure of the documents. In practice, this means that documents from the same collection need not have the same set of fields or structure and that common fields in a collection of documents can carry different types of data.

As seen in our example, using Mongoose to map our database standardizes the documents of the same schema. This ensures that instances of the model that compiled the schema will always have the same data type attributes specified in the schema.

Summary

We finished our chapter with a lot of new information about the whole process to create a Node server and run web applications.

We covered the essential topics to start the development of our example application, starting with our Node server, NPM, and how to install modules and dependencies, import modules with `require`, and export modules to use later with `module.exports`. We saw that MongoDB has a GUI administration interface and learned some command lines to help us in our future queries.

We learned the power of the Express framework, where we can build simple to complex web applications and also how to use object modeling with the Mongoose module to create schemas and models for our data. But don't worry if you do not understand all the concepts here; we will discuss them in more detail in the next chapters.

Our journey has just begun; we'll see another bunch of tools and get our hands dirty with a lot of code to start building our API in the following chapters. In the next chapter, we will see how the API works, some lines about the RESTful architecture, and how to start the development using Yeoman generators.

3
API with MongoDB and Node.js

This chapter will focus directly on the code, so we can have the necessary understanding to build a solid foundation for our API. Our main aim is to discuss the techniques to build rich web applications, with the SPA approach.

Application Programming Interface (**API**) is the set of programming standards that enables us to build applications. Their usage is not so evident to the user using the application. The API is the *engine* of the application; an interface that runs behind it all. While you might benefit from an application or website, your API can be connected to several other systems and applications. With APIs, applications talk to each other without user intervention.

We will be covering the following topics in this chapter:

- The working of an API
- Boilerplates and generators
- The speakers API concept
- Creating the `package.json` file
- The Node server with server.js
- The model with the Mongoose schema
- Defining the API routes
- Using MongoDB in the cloud
- Inserting data with the Postman Chrome extension

The working of an API

An API works through communication between different codes, thus defining specific behavior of certain objects on an interface. That is, the API will connect several functions on one website (such as search, images, news, authentications, and so on) to enable it to be used in other applications.

Operating systems also have APIs, and they still have the same function. Windows, for example, has APIs such as the Win16 API, Win32 API, or Telephony API, in all its versions. When you run a program that involves some process of the operating system, it is likely that we make a connection with one or more Windows APIs. To clarify the concept of an API, we will give go through some examples of how it works.

On Windows, it works on an application that uses the system clock to display the same function within the program. It then associates a behavior to a given clock time in another application, for example, using the Time/Clock API from Windows to use the clock functionality on your own application.

Another example, is when you use the Android SDK to build mobile applications. When you use the device GPS, you are interacting with the API (`android.location`) to display the user location on the map through another API, in this case, Google Maps API.

The following is the API example:

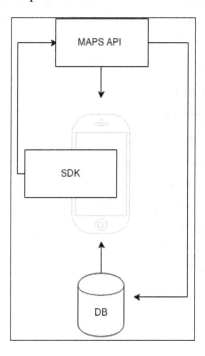

When it comes to web APIs, the functionality can be even greater. There are many services that provide their code, so that they can be used on other websites. Perhaps, the best example is the Facebook API. Several other websites use this service within their pages, for instance a like button, share, or even authentication.

> An API is a set of programming patterns and instructions to access a software application based on the Web.

So, when you access a page of a beer store in your town, you can log in with your Facebook account. This is accomplished through the API. Using it, software developers and web programmers can create beautiful programs and pages filled with content for their users.

Boilerplates and generators

On a MEAN stack environment, our ecosystem is infinitely diverse, and we can find excellent alternatives to start the construction of our API. At hand, we have simple boilerplates to complex code generators that can be used with other tools in an integrated way, or even alone.

Boilerplates are usually a group of tested code that provides the basic structure to the main goal, that is to create a foundation of a web project. Besides saving us from common tasks such as assembling the basic structure of the code and organizing the files, boilerplates already have a number of scripts to make life easier for the frontend.

Let's describe some alternatives that we consider as good starting points for the development of APIs with the Express framework, MongoDB database, Node server, and AngularJS for the frontend.

Some more accentuated knowledge of JavaScript might be necessary for the complete understanding of the concepts covered here; so we will try to make them as clearly as possible.

It is important to note that everything is still very new when we talk about Node and all its ecosystems, and factors such as scalability, performance, and maintenance are still major risk factors. Bearing in mind also that languages such as Ruby on Rails, Scala, and the Play framework have a higher reputation in building large and maintainable web applications, but without a doubt, Node and JavaScript will conquer your space very soon.

That being said, we present some alternatives for the initial kickoff with MEAN, but remember that our main focus is on SPA and not directly on MEAN stack.

Hackathon starter

Hackathon is highly recommended for a quick start to develop with Node. This is because the boilerplate has the main necessary characteristics to develop applications with the Express framework to build RESTful APIs, as it has no MVC/MVVM frontend framework as a standard but just the Bootstrap UI framework. Thus, you are free to choose the framework of your choice, as you will not need to refactor it to meet your needs.

Other important characteristics are the use of the latest version of the Express framework, heavy use of Jade templates and some middleware such as Passport—a Node module to manage authentication with various social network sites such as Twitter, Facebook, APIs for LinkedIn, GitHub, Last.fm, Foursquare, and many more.

They provide the necessary boilerplate code to start your projects very fast, and as we said before, it is very simple to install; just clone the Git open source repository:

```
git clone --depth=1 https://github.com/sahat/hackathon-starter.git
myproject
```

Run the NPM install command inside the project folder:

```
npm install
```

Then, start the Node server:

```
node app.js
```

Remember, it is very important to have your local database up and running, in this case MongoDB, otherwise the command `node app.js` will return the error: **Error connecting to database: failed to connect to [localhost: 27017]**

You can check for more details at: `https://github.com/sahat/hackathon-starter`

MEAN.io or MEAN.JS

This is perhaps the most popular and currently available boilerplate. MEAN.JS is a fork of the original project MEAN.io; both are open source, with a very peculiar similarity, both have the same author. You can check for more details at `http://meanjs.org/`.

However, there are some differences. We consider MEAN.JS to be a more complete and robust environment. It has a structure of directories, better organized, subdivided modules, and better scalability by adopting a vertical modules development.

To install it, follow the same steps as previously:

1. Clone the repository to your machine:
   ```
   git clone https://github.com/meanjs/mean.git
   ```

2. Go to the installation directory and type on your terminal:
   ```
   npm install
   ```

3. Finally, execute the application; this time with the Grunt.js command:
   ```
   grunt
   ```

4. If you are on Windows, type the following command:
   ```
   grunt.cmd
   ```

Now, you have your app up and running on your localhost.

The most common problem when we need to scale a SPA is undoubtedly the structure of directories and how we manage all of the frontend JavaScript files and HTML templates using MVC/MVVM. Later, we will see an alternative to deal with this on a large-scale application; for now, let's see the module structure adopted by MEAN.JS:

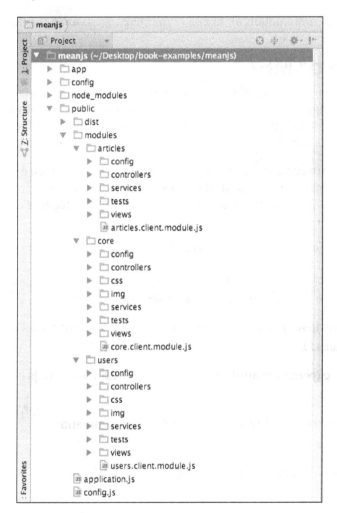

Note that MEAN.JS leaves more flexibility to the AngularJS framework to deal with the MVC approach for the frontend application, as we can see inside the **public** folder. Also, note the modules approach; each module has its own structure, keeping some conventions for `controllers`, `services`, `views`, `config`, and `tests`. This is very useful for team development, so keep all the structure well organized. It is a complete solution that makes use of additional modules such as `passport`, `swig`, `mongoose`, `karma`, among others.

The Passport module

Some things about the Passport module must be said; it can be defined as a simple, unobtrusive authentication module. It is a powerful middleware to use with Node; it is very flexible and also modular. It can also adapt easily within applications that use the Express.

It has more than 140 alternative authentications and support session persistence; it is very lightweight and extremely simple to be implemented. It provides us with all the necessary structure for authentication, redirects, and validations, and hence it is possible to use the username and password of social networks such as Facebook, Twitter, and others.

The following is a simple example of how to use local authentication:

```
var passport = require('passport'),
LocalStrategy = require('passport-local').Strategy,
User = require('mongoose').model('User');

module.exports = function() {
// Use local strategy
passport.use(new LocalStrategy({
  usernameField: 'username',
  passwordField: 'password'
},
function(username, password, done) {
  User.findOne({
    username: username
  },
function(err, user) {
  if (err) {
  return done(err);
  }
  if (!user) {
    return done(null, false, {
    message: 'Unknown user'
    });
  }
  if (!user.authenticate(password)) {
    return done(null, false, {
    message: 'Invalid password'
    });
  }
return done(null, user);
});
}
));
};
```

Here's a sample screenshot of the login page using the MEAN.JS boilerplate with the Passport module:

Back to the boilerplates topic; most boilerplates and generators already have the Passport module installed and ready to be configured. Moreover, it has a code generator so that it can be used with Yeoman, which is another essential frontend tool to be added to your tool belt.

Yeoman is the most popular code generator for scaffold for modern web applications; it's easy to use and it has a lot of generators such as Backbone, Angular, Karma, and Ember to mention a few. More information can be found at http://yeoman.io/.

Generators

Generators are for the frontend as gem is for Ruby on Rails. We can create the foundation for any type of application, using available generators.

Here's a console output from a Yeoman generator:

```
MacBook-Pro-de-fernando:angular-fullstack-yo fernandomonteiro$ yo angular-fullstack


      ------
     |      |
     |--(o)--|    .----------------------------.
     `---------'  |   Welcome to Yeoman,       |
     ( _'U'_ )    |  ladies and gentlemen!     |
     /___A___\    '----------------------------'
      |  ~  |
    __'.___.'__
  `  |° ´ Y `


Out of the box I include Bootstrap and some AngularJS recommended modules.

[?] Would you like to use Sass (with Compass)? No
[?] Would you like to include Twitter Bootstrap? No
[?] Which modules would you like to include? angular-resource.js, angular-cookies.js, angular-sanitize.js,
ar-route.js
[?] Would you like to include MongoDB with Mongoose? No
   create app/styles/main.css
   create app/scripts/controllers/navbar.js
   create app/views/index.html
   create app/views/partials/main.html
   create app/views/partials/navbar.html
   create app/views/404.html
   create bower.json
   create package.json
   create Gruntfile.js
   create app/images/yeoman.png
   create server.js
   create lib/.jshintrc
   create lib/controllers/api.js
   create lib/controllers/index.js
   create lib/routes.js
   create test/server/thing/api.js
   create lib/config/express.js
   create lib/config/config.js
   create lib/config/env/all.js
   create lib/config/env/development.js
```

It is important to bear in mind that we can solve almost all our problems using existing generators in our community. However, if you cannot find the generator you need, you can create your own and make it available to the entire community, such as what has been done with RubyGems by the Rails community.

RubyGem, or simply gem, is a library of reusable Ruby files, labeled with a name and a version (a file called gemspec).

 Keep in mind the **Don't Repeat Yourself** (**DRY**) concept; always try to reuse an existing block of code. Don't reinvent the wheel.

One of the great advantages of using a code generator structure is that many of the generators that we have currently, have plenty of options for the installation process. With them, you can choose whether or not to use many alternatives/frameworks that usually accompany the generator.

The Express generator

Another good option is the Express generator, which can be found at
`https://github.com/expressjs/generator`.

In all versions up to Express Version 4, the generator was already pre-installed and
served as a scaffold to begin development. However, in the current version, it was
removed and now must be installed as a supplement.

They provide us with the `express` command directly in terminal and are quite
useful to start the basic settings for utilization of the framework, as we can see in
the following commands:

```
create : .
create : ./package.json
create : ./app.js
create : ./public
create : ./public/javascripts
create : ./public/images
create : ./public/stylesheets
create : ./public/stylesheets/style.css
create : ./routes
create : ./routes/index.js
create : ./routes/users.js
create : ./views
create : ./views/index.jade
create : ./views/layout.jade
create : ./views/error.jade
create : ./bin
create : ./bin/www


install dependencies:
  $ cd . && npm install

run the app:
  $ DEBUG=express-generator ./bin/www
```

Very similar to the Rails scaffold, we can observe the creation of the directory and files, including the `public`, `routes`, and `views` folders that are the basis of any application using Express.

Note the `npm install` command; it installs all dependencies provided with the `package.json` file, created as follows:

```
{
  "name": "express-generator",
  "version": "0.0.1",
  "private": true,
  "scripts": {
    "start": "node ./bin/www"
  },
  "dependencies": {
    "express": "~4.2.0",
    "static-favicon": "~1.0.0",
    "morgan": "~1.0.0",
    "cookie-parser": "~1.0.1",
    "body-parser": "~1.0.0",
    "debug": "~0.7.4",
    "jade": "~1.3.0"
  }
}
```

This has a simple and effective `package.json` file to build web applications with the Express framework.

The speakers API concept

Let's go directly to build the example API. To be more realistic, let's write a user story similar to a backlog list in agile methodologies.

Let's understand what problem we need to solve by the API.

The user history

We need a web application to manage speakers on a conference event. The main task is to store the following speaker information on an API:

- Name
- Company
- Track title
- Description
- A speaker picture
- Schedule presentation

For now, we need to add, edit, and delete speakers. It is a simple CRUD function using exclusively the API with JSON format files.

Creating the package.json file

Although not necessarily required at this time, we recommend that you install the Webstorm IDE, as we'll use it throughout the book.

Note that we are using the Webstorm IDE with an integrated environment with terminal, GitHub version control, and Grunt to ease our development. However, you are absolutely free to choose your own environment.

> From now on, when we mention terminal, we are referring to terminal Integrated WebStorm, but you can access it directly by the chosen independent editor, terminal for Mac and Linux and Command Prompt for Windows.

Webstorm is very useful when you are using a Windows environment, because Windows Command Prompt does not have the facility to copy and paste like Mac OS X on the terminal window.

Initiating the JSON file

Follow the steps to initiate the JSON file:

1. Create a blank folder and name it as `conference-api`, open your terminal, and place the command:

    ```
    npm init
    ```

This command will walk you through creating a `package.json` file with the baseline configuration for our application. Also, this file is the heart of our application; we can control all the dependencies' versions and other important things like author, GitHub repositories, development dependencies, type of license, testing commands, and much more.

2. Almost all commands are questions that guide you to the final process, so when we are done, we'll have a `package.json` file very similar to this:

```
{
  "name": "conference-api",
  "version": "0.0.1",
  "description": "Sample Conference Web Application",
  "main": "server.js",
  "scripts": {
    "test": "test"
  },
  "keywords": [
    "api"
  ],
  "author": "your name here",
  "license": "MIT"
}
```

3. Now, we need to add the necessary dependencies, such as Node modules, which we will use in our process. You can do this in two ways, either directly via terminal as we did here, or by editing the `package.json` file. Let's see how it works on the terminal first; let's start with the Express framework. Open your terminal in the `api` folder and type the following command:

```
npm install express@4.0.0 --save
```

This command installs the Express module, in this case, Express Version 4, and updates the `package.json` file and also creates dependencies automatically, as we can see:

```
{
  "name": "conference-api",
  "version": "0.0.1",
  "description": "Sample Conference Web Application",
  "main": "server.js",
  "scripts": {
```

```
    "test": "test"
  },
  "keywords": [
    "api"
  ],
  "author": "your name here",
  "license": "MIT",
  "dependencies": {
    "express": "^4.0.0"
  }
}
```

4. Now, let's add more dependencies directly in the package.json file.
   Open the file in your editor and add the following lines:

```
{
  "name": "conference-api",
  "version": "0.0.1",
  "description": "Sample Conference Web Application",
  "main": "server.js",
  "scripts": {
    "test": "test"
  },
  "keywords": [
    "api"
  ],
  "author": "your name here",
  "license": "MIT",
  "engines": {
        "node": "0.8.4",
        "npm": "1.1.49"
  },
  "dependencies": {
    "body-parser": "^1.0.1",
    "express": "^4.0.0",
    "method-override": "^1.0.0",
    "mongoose": "^3.6.13",
    "morgan": "^1.0.0",
    "nodemon": "^1.2.0"
  },
}
```

> It's very important when you deploy your application using some services such as Travis Cl or Heroku hosting company. It's always good to set up the Node environment.

5. Open the terminal again and type the command:

   `npm install`

You can actually install the dependencies in two different ways, either directly into the directory of your application or globally with the `-g` command. This way, you will have the modules installed to use them in any application.

When using this option, make sure that you are the administrator of the user machine, as this command requires special permissions to write to the root directory of the user.

At the end of the process, we'll have all Node modules that we need for this project; we just need one more action.

Let's place our code over a version control, in our case Git.

> More information about the Git can be found at `http://git-scm.com/`; however, you can use any version control as subversion or another.

We recommend using Git, as we will need it later to deploy our application in the cloud, more specificly, on Heroku cloud hosting.

At this time, our project folder must have the same structure as that of the example shown here:

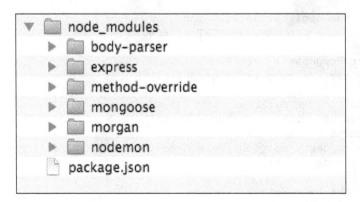

We must point out the utilization of an important module called the `Nodemon` module. Whenever a file changes it restarts the server automatically; otherwise, you will have to restart the server manually every time you make a change to a file, especially in a development environment that is extremely useful, as it constantly updates our files.

Node server with server.js

With this structure formed, we will start the creation of the server itself, which is the creation of a main JavaScript file.

The most common name used is `server.js`, but it is also very common to use the `app.js` name, especially in older versions.

Let's add this file to the root folder of the project and we will start with the basic server settings.

There are many ways to configure our server, and probably you'll find the best one for yourself. As we are still in the initial process, we keep only the basics.

Open your editor and type in the following code:

```
// Import the Modules installed to our server
var express     = require('express');
var bodyParser = require('body-parser');

// Start the Express web framework
var app         = express();

// configure app
app.use(bodyParser());

// where the application will run
var port        = process.env.PORT || 8080;

// Import Mongoose
var mongoose    = require('mongoose');

// connect to our database
// you can use your own MongoDB installation at: mongodb://127.0.0.1/
databasename
mongoose.connect('mongodb://username:password@kahana.mongohq.
com:10073/node-api');

// Start the Node Server
app.listen(port);
console.log('Magic happens on port ' + port);
```

Realize that the line-making connection with MongoDB on our localhost is commented, because we are using an instance of MongoDB in the cloud. In our case, we use MongoHQ, a MongoDB-hosting service. Later on, will see how to connect with MongoHQ.

Model with the Mongoose schema

Now, let's create our model, using the Mongoose schema to map our speakers on MongoDB.

```
// Import the Mongoose module.
var mongoose      = require('mongoose');
var Schema        = mongoose.Schema;

// Set the data types, properties and default values to our Schema.
var SpeakerSchema     = new Schema({
    name:             { type: String, default: '' },
    company:          { type: String, default: '' },
    title:            { type: String, default: '' },
    description:      { type: String, default: '' },
    picture:          { type: String, default: '' },
    schedule:         { type: String, default: '' },
    createdOn:        { type: Date,   default: Date.now}
});
module.exports = mongoose.model('Speaker', SpeakerSchema);
```

Note that on the first line, we added the Mongoose module using the `require()` function.

Our schema is pretty simple; on the left-hand side, we have the property name and on the right-hand side, the data type. We also we set the default value to nothing, but if you want, you can set a different value.

The next step is to save this file to our project folder. For this, let's create a new directory named `server`; then inside this, create another folder called `models` and save the file as `speaker.js`. At this point, our folder looks like this:

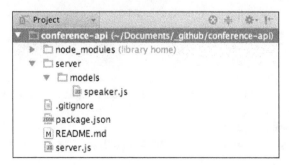

The README.md file is used for GitHub; as we are using the Git version control, we host our files on GitHub.

Defining the API routes

One of the most important aspects of our API are routes that we take to create, read, update, and delete our speakers.

Our routes are based on the HTTP verb used to access our API, as shown in the following examples:

- To create record, use the POST verb
- To read record, use the GET verb
- To update record, use the PUT verb
- To delete records, use the DELETE verb

So, our routes will be as follows:

Routes	Verb and Action
/api/speakers	GET retrieves speaker's records
/api/speakers/	POST inserts speakers' record
/api/speakers/:speaker_id	GET retrieves a single record
/api/speakers/:speaker_id	PUT updates a single record
/api/speakers/:speaker_id	DELETE deletes a single record

Configuring the API routes:

1. Let's start defining the route and a common message for all requests:

```
var Speaker     = require('./server/models/speaker');

// Defining the Routes for our API

// Start the Router
var router = express.Router();

// A simple middleware to use for all Routes and Requests
router.use(function(req, res, next) {
// Give some message on the console
console.log('An action was performed by the server.');
```

```
// Is very important using the next() function, without this the
Route stops here.
next();
});


// Default message when access the API folder through the browser
router.get('/', function(req, res) {
// Give some Hello there message
res.json({ message: 'Hello SPA, the API is working!' });
});
```

2. Now, let's add the route to insert the speakers when the HTTP verb is POST:

```
// When accessing the speakers Routes
router.route('/speakers')


// create a speaker when the method passed is POST
.post(function(req, res) {


// create a new instance of the Speaker model
var speaker = new Speaker();


// set the speakers properties (comes from the request)
  speaker.name = req.body.name;
  speaker.company = req.body.company;
  speaker.title = req.body.title;
  speaker.description = req.body.description;
  speaker.picture = req.body.picture;
  speaker.schedule = req.body.schedule;


// save the data received
  speaker.save(function(err) {
    if (err)
      res.send(err);


// give some success message
  res.json({ message: 'speaker successfully created!' });
  });
})
```

3. For the HTTP GET method, we need this:

```
// get all the speakers when a method passed is GET
.get(function(req, res) {
  Speaker.find(function(err, speakers) {
    if (err)
```

```
        res.send(err);

    res.json(speakers);
  });
});
```

Note that in the `res.json()` function, we send all the object speakers as an answer. Now, we will see the use of different routes in the following steps:

1. To retrieve a single record, we need to pass `speaker_id`, as shown in our previous table, so let's build this function:

```
// on accessing speaker Route by id
router.route('/speakers/:speaker_id')

// get the speaker by id
.get(function(req, res) {
  Speaker.findById(req.params.speaker_id, function(err,
    speaker) {
    if (err)
      res.send(err);
      res.json(speaker);
    });
})
```

2. To update a specific record, we use the PUT HTTP verb and then insert the function:

```
// update the speaker by id
.put(function(req, res) {
  Speaker.findById(req.params.speaker_id, function(err,
    speaker) {

    if (err)
      res.send(err);

// set the speakers properties (comes from the request)
    speaker.name = req.body.name;
    speaker.company = req.body.company;
    speaker.title = req.body.title;
    speaker.description = req.body.description;
    speaker.picture = req.body.picture;
    speaker.schedule = req.body.schedule;

// save the data received
    speaker.save(function(err) {
```

```
    if (err)
      res.send(err);
      // give some success message
      res.json({ message: 'speaker successfully
      updated!'});
    });

    });
  })
```

3. To delete a specific record by its id:

```
// delete the speaker by id
.delete(function(req, res) {
  Speaker.remove({
    _id: req.params.speaker_id
  }, function(err, speaker) {
    if (err)
      res.send(err);

// give some success message
  res.json({ message: 'speaker successfully deleted!' });
  });
});
```

4. Finally, register the Routes on our `server.js` file:

```
// register the route
app.use('/api', router);
```

All necessary work to configure the basic CRUD routes has been done, and we are ready to run our server and begin creating and updating our database.

Open a small parenthesis here, for a quick step-by-step process to introduce another tool to create a database using MongoDB in the cloud.

There are many companies that provide this type of service but we will not go into individual merits here; you can choose your preference. We chose Compose (formerly MongoHQ) that has a free sandbox for development, which is sufficient for our examples.

Using MongoDB in the cloud

Today, we have many options to work with MongoDB, from in-house services to hosting companies that provide **Platform as a Service (PaaS)** and **Software as a Service (SaaS)**.

We will present a solution called **Database as a Service (DbaaS)** that provides database services for highly scalable web applications.

Here's a simple step-by-step process to start using a MongoDB instance with a cloud service:

1. Go to `https://www.compose.io/`.
2. Create your free account.
3. On your dashboard panel, click on **add Database**.
4. On the right-hand side, choose **Sandbox Database**.
5. Name your database as `node-api`.
6. Add a user to your database.
7. Go back to your database title, click on **admin**.
8. Copy the connection string.
9. The string connection looks like this:

   `mongodb://<user>:<password>@kahana.mongohq.com:10073/node-api`.

Let's edit the `server.js` file using the following steps:

1. Place your own connection string to the `Mongoose.connect()` function.
2. Open your terminal and input the command:

   `nodemon server.js`

3. Open your browser and place `http://localhost:8080/api`.
4. You will see a message like this in the browser:

   {
   Hello SPA, the API is working!
   }

5. Remember the `api` folder was defined on the `server.js` file when we registered the routes:

   `app.use('/api', router);`

6. But, if you try to access `http://localhost:8080/api/speakers`, you must have something like this: []

   This is an empty array, because we haven't input any data into MongoDB.

 We use an extension for the Chrome browser called JSONView. This way, we can view the formatted and readable JSON files. You can install this for free from the Chrome Web Store.

Inserting data with Postman

To solve our empty database and before we create our frontend interface, let's add some data with the Chrome extension Postman. By the way, it's a very useful browser interface to work with RESTful APIs.

As we already know that our database is empty, our first task is to insert a record. To do so, perform the following steps:

1. Open Postman and enter `http://localhost:8080/api/speakers`. Select the **x-www-form-urlencoded** option and add the properties of our model:

```
var SpeakerSchema    = new Schema({
    name:           { type: String, default: '' },
    company:        { type: String, default: '' },
    title:          { type: String, default: '' },
    description:    { type: String, default: '' },
    picture:        { type: String, default: '' },
    schedule:       { type: String, default: '' },
    createdOn:      { type: Date,    default: Date.now}
});
```

2. Now, click on the blue button at the end to send the request.

3. With everything going as expected, you should see **message: speaker successfully created!** at the bottom of the screen, as shown in the following screenshot:

4. Now, let's try `http://localhost:8080/api/speakers` in the browser again.

5. Now, we have a JSON file like this, instead of an empty array:

```
{
    "_id": "53a38ffd2cd34a7904000007",
    "__v": 0,
    "createdOn": "2014-06-20T02:20:31.384Z",
    "schedule": "10:20",
    "picture": "fernando.jpg",
    "description": "Lorem ipsum dolor sit amet, consectetur
        adipisicing elit, sed do eiusmod...",
    "title": "MongoDB",
    "company": "Newaeonweb",
    "name": "Fernando Monteiro"
}
```

6. When performing the same action on Postman, we see the same result, as shown in the following screenshot:

7. Go back to Postman, copy _id from the preceding JSON file and add to the end of the `http://localhost:8080/api/speakers/53a38ffd2cd3 4a7904000005` URL and click on **Send**. You will see the same object on the screen.

8. Now, let's test the method to update the object. In this case, change the method to **PUT** on Postman and click on **Send**. The output is shown in the following screenshot:

9. Note that on the left-hand side, we have three methods under **History**; now, let's perform the last operation and delete the record. This is very simple to perform; just keep the same URL, change the method on Postman to **DELETE**, and click on **Send**. Finally, we have the last method executed successfully, as shown in the following screenshot:

Take a look at your terminal, you can see four messages that are the same: **An action was performed by the server**. We configured this message in the `server.js` file when we were dealing with all routes of our API.

```
router.use(function(req, res, next) {
// Give some message on the console
console.log('An action was performed by the server.');
// Is very important using the next() function, without this the Route
stops here.
next();
});
```

This way, we can monitor all interactions that take place at our API.

Now that we have our API properly tested and working, we can start the development of the interface that will handle all this data.

Summary

We have now ended yet another chapter with a storm of information and good practices. We have covered almost all modules of the Node ecosystem to develop the RESTful API.

Our journey is still just the beginning. We have many issues ahead and we will treat them the same way: by always prioritizing best practices and using open source alternatives to solve our problems.

In the next chapter, we will show how we can build the interface of our application using a few frameworks to speed up frontend development with the Responsive boilerplate. We will also discuss Pure CSS, how to refactor the API using an Express generator and how to set up routes, and user authentication with Passport.

4
Creating a Conference Web Application

This chapter will devote time and attention to refactoring and building the web application.

Nowadays, the workflow for a frontend developer can be very tricky if you do not use the right tools, and here in this book we will use some of the most important modern tools for fast and simple development.

At first glance, everything seems too complicated; we must remember that our choices lead us to different paths and that there is more than one way to develop an application. Nothing is better than practicing in order to choose the best way that will be useful to you.

In this chapter, we'll see some very interesting stuff such as the frontend dependencies manager known as Bower, how to start an application from scratch using the Express generator, adding secure authentication with Passport, and much, much more. The topics we will cover are:

- Rebuilding the API
- Adding the Passport middleware
- Dealing with routes
- Templates with Embedded JavaScript
- Bower leading frontend dependencies
- Pure CSS and Responsive Boilerplate for the frontend style

Rebuilding the API

The rebuilding process is divided into two parts: the first to have a solid base structure of directories and the second to add some more folders and files with the purpose of making our application as modular and scalable as possible.

Getting the baseline structure

To start with, we will create a new folder called `conference-api`. Going forward, we will refer to this folder only as the root folder. So, you already know that we are referring to the application root directory. The first thing to do is start the Express scaffold generator; to do this open the terminal on the root folder and type:

```
express --ejs
```

The `ejs` option stands for **Embedded JavaScript (EJS)**, and with this command, we change the standard library `Jade` to `ejs` for the views' templates.

 You can read more about Embedded JavaScript at http://www.embeddedjs.com/.

At this stage, you must have the following default scaffold, as shown in the following screenshot:

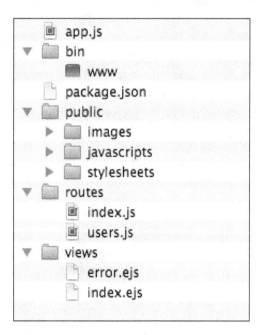

Changing the initialization process

As we saw in the previous chapter and in the previous screenshot, the generator creates a `bin` folder. In this folder, we have a file called www; this file is responsible for running the server for the application. However, instead of using the default command, `npm start`, on each time we need to execute the server to test and develop the application. We will make some changes on how to start the server. To do this, follow these steps:

1. Delete the `bin` folder.

2. Open the `app.js` file on the root folder and place the following code at the end of the file:

```
app.set('port', process.env.PORT || 3000);
var server = app.listen(app.get('port'), function() {
    console.log('Express server listening on port ' + server.
address().port);
});
```

3. Rename the file `app.js` to `server.js`.

Now, let's check the result of these changes and start the server using the following command on your terminal:

`node server`

You will see the **Express server listening on port 3000** message on your terminal. This means that if you open your browser and type http: // localhost: 3000, you will see a welcome message from the Express framework.

The `node server` command is the most common command to initialize a Node.js application.

To stop the server, press *Ctrl + C.*

Changing the directory structure

Now, let's make some changes in the directory structure. Our aim is to prepare the application for a division of responsibilities, creating a directory named `server` that will contain all the application backend code; to be more specific, the API code.

Let's use the following steps to change the directory structure:

1. In the root folder, create a new folder and name it `server`.

2. Move the `routes` and `views` folders to the newly created `server` folder. We still need to accomplish an important task. When changing directories, it also is necessary to change some paths for the `views` and `routes` folders within the `server.js` file.

3. Open the `server.js` file, and update the route path inside the `require()` function from the `routes` and `users` variables; your code must look like this:

```
// Setup Routes
var routes = require('./server/routes/index');
var users = require('./server/routes/users');
```

4. Open the `server.js` file, go to the `view engine setup` commented line, and change to the following code:

```
// view engine setup
app.set('views', path.join(__dirname, 'server/views'));
```

5. Now, let's check whether everything went as expected up to here; type the following command:

```
node server.js
```

6. Open your browser and go to `http://localhost:3000`.

If successful, we will see the home page of our application with the welcome message from the Express framework again.

One of the advantages of using the Express generator is that it comes with all the basic modules configured to run our application, avoiding writing many lines of code. With only this small change, you already have in hand a solid scaffold to start developing applications with Node and the Express framework.

Our folder will look like the following screenshot:

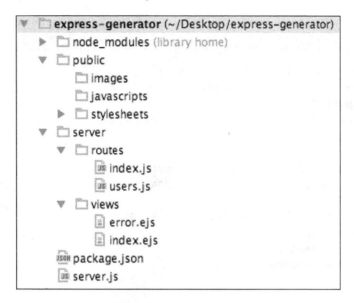

Inserting new folders and files

Let's perform a few more steps to accomplish the modularization of our application. Here, we will create two directories; one to store the configuration file and another to store the application's models for the backend by performing the following steps:

1. Add a new folder called `config` to the `server` folder.

2. Add a new folder called `models` to the `server` folder.

3. Right now, we need to add the `speaker.js` model file to the `models` folders and `speakers` route to the `routes` folder. As we have already created these files in the previous chapter, you can just copy them and insert them into each folder. The `speaker.js` model file looks like the following:

```
var mongoose = require('mongoose');
var Schema = mongoose.Schema;

var SpeakerSchema    = new Schema({
    name:           { type: String, default: '' },
    company:        { type: String, default: '' },
    title:          { type: String, default: '' },
    description:    { type: String, default: '' },
    picture:        { type: String, default: '' },
    schedule:       { type: String, default: '' },
    createdOn:      { type: Date,   default: Date.now}
```

```
});

module.exports = mongoose.model('Speaker', SpeakerSchema);

The speakers.js route code:
var express = require('express');
var router = express.Router();
// Import Speakers Model
var Speaker      = require('../models/speaker');

/* GET all users. */
router.get('/', function(req, res) {
  //res.json({ message: 'Hello SPA, the API is working!'
  });
  Speaker.find(function(err, speakers) {
    if (err)
      res.send(err);
      res.json(speakers);
  });

});

/* GET specific users by id. */
router.get('/:speaker_id', function(req, res) {

  Speaker.findById(req.params.speaker_id, function(err, speaker) {
    if (err)
      res.send(err);
      res.json(speaker);
  });

});

/* PUT users */
router.post('/', function(req, res) {
  // create a new instance of the Speaker model
  var speaker = new Speaker();

  // set the speakers properties (comes from the request)
  speaker.name = req.body.name;
  speaker.company = req.body.company;
  speaker.title = req.body.title;
  speaker.description = req.body.description;
  speaker.picture = req.body.picture;
```

```
    speaker.schedule = req.body.schedule;

    // save the data received
    speaker.save(function(err) {
      if (err)
        res.send(err);

        // give some success message
        res.json({ message: 'speaker successfully created!'
        });
    });

  });

  /* UPDATE specific users by id. */
  router.put('/:speaker_id', function(req, res) {

    Speaker.findById(req.params.speaker_id, function(err,
    speaker) {
      if (err)
        res.send(err);

        // set the speakers properties (comes from the
        request)
        speaker.name = req.body.name;
        speaker.company = req.body.company;
        speaker.title = req.body.title;
        speaker.description = req.body.description;
        speaker.picture = req.body.picture;
        speaker.schedule = req.body.schedule;

        // save the data received
        speaker.save(function(err) {
          if (err)
            res.send(err);

            // give some success message
            res.json({ message: 'speaker successfully
            updated!' });
        });

    });

  });
```

```
/* DELETE specific users by id. */
router.delete('/:speaker_id', function(req, res) {

  Speaker.remove({
    _id: req.params.speaker_id
  }, function(err, speaker) {
      if (err)
        res.send(err);

        // give some success message
        res.json({ message: 'speaker successfully
        deleted!'});
  });

});

// Exports all the routes to router variable
module.exports = router;
```

Remember, every time you add a new route file, you must set up the routes on the `server.js` file.

4. Add the path to the `speakers.js` route on the `server.js` file after the routes setup, as shown here:

```
// Setup Routes
var routes = require('./server/routes/index');
var users = require('./server/routes/users');
var speakers = require('./server/routes/speakers');
```

Without this action, the application won't initialize the route and we won't be able to use it later. Now, the last action to perform in this section is to tell the application to use the route.

5. Add the highlighted code to the end of the `app.use()` function, as shown in the following code:

```
app.use('/', routes);
app.use('/users', users);
app.use('/api/speakers', speakers);
```

Creating the configuration file

In this section, we will add a database configuration to the `server.js` file.

1. Create a new file inside the `config` folder and name it `config.js`.

2. Place the following code in the `config.js` file:

```
// Database URL
module.exports = {
    // Uncomment to connect with MongoDB on Cloud
    // 'url' : 'mongodb://username:password@kahana.mongohq.
com:10073/node-
api'
    'url' : 'localhost/conferenceDB'
};
```

3. Open the `server.js` file and add the database connection after the routes setup:

```
// Database configuration
var config = require('./server/config/config.js');
// connect to our database
mongoose.connect(config.url);
```

   Another important step is to add some friendly warning message if the connection fails for some reason.

4. Add the following code right after `mongoose.connect(config.url)`:

```
// Check if MongoDB is running
mongoose.connection.on('error', function() {
    console.error('MongoDB Connection Error. Make sure
    MongoDB is running.');
});
```

   Note that we have a `mongoose.connect` function already used in the previous chapter. However, here we need to install this dependency and add it to the `server.js` file, as we are starting from scratch using the Express generator.

5. Open your terminal and type the following command:

   npm install mongoose --save

   The `--save` option will add the Mongoose dependency to our `package.json` file.

   To use the Mongoose middleware, we need to import it to the `server.js` file.

6. Add the following highlighted code to the `server.js` file.

```
var express = require('express');
var path = require('path');
var favicon = require('static-favicon');
var logger = require('morgan');
var cookieParser = require('cookie-parser');
var bodyParser = require('body-parser');
var mongoose = require('mongoose');
```

Now, the first stage is complete using the Express generator. To check whether everything went well, let's start the server and check the `http://localhost:3000/api/speakers` URL on the browser.

As you can see, we get an empty page; this is because we didn't add any data to MongoDB at this stage. However, if you check your terminal window, you will have the **GET /api/speakers 200 xxms - 2b** message. This indicates that the request was successful.

Adding the Passport middleware

As mentioned earlier, we use Passport to deal with user authentication in our API. Here, we will see how to use and store sessions and encrypt a user password to maintain a secure authentication.

First of all, let's install and save the Passport middleware to the application:

1. Open the terminal and type the following command:

   ```
   npm install passport passport-local --save
   ```

2. Place the following code after the `app` express variable:

   ```
   // Passport configuration
   require('./server/config/passport')(passport);
   ```

3. Now, we need to create a `passport.js` file and the necessary code inside the `config` folder. We can name this file with any name. However, to demonstrate the use of the `passport` module, we use the same name from the module. Create a `passport.js` file in the `config` folder and place the following code:

   ```
   // Import passport module
   var LocalStrategy = require('passport-local').Strategy;

   // Import the user model
   ```

```javascript
var User = require('../../server/models/user');

module.exports = function(passport) {
  // passport setup
  // serialize user
  passport.serializeUser(function(user, done) {
    done(null, user.id);
    });
  // deserialize user
  passport.deserializeUser(function(id, done) {
    User.findById(id, function(err, user) {
      done(err, user);
      });
  });
  // Configure local login strategy
  passport.use('local-login', new LocalStrategy({
    // change default username and password, to email and
    password
    usernameField : 'email',
    passwordField : 'password',
    passReqToCallback : true
  },
  function(req, email, password, done) {
    if (email) {
      // format to lower-case
      email = email.toLowerCase();
    }
  // asynchronous
  process.nextTick(function() {
    User.findOne({ 'local.email' :  email }, function(err,
      user) {
        // if errors
        if (err) {
          return done(err);
        }
    // check errors and bring the messages
      if (!user) {
        // third parameter is a flash warning message
        return done(null, false, req.flash('loginMessage',
        'No user found.'));
      }
      if (!user.validPassword(password)) {
        return done(null, false, req.flash('loginMessage',
        'Warning! Wrong password.'));
```

```
      } else {
        // everything ok, get user
        return done(null, user);
      }
    });
  });
}));
// Configure signup local strategy
passport.use('local-signup', new LocalStrategy({
  // change default username and password, to email and
  password
  usernameField : 'email',
  passwordField : 'password',
  passReqToCallback : true
},
function(req, email, password, done) {
  if (email) {
    // format to lower-case
    email = email.toLowerCase();
  }
// asynchronous
process.nextTick(function() {
  // if the user is not already logged in:
    if (!req.user) {
      User.findOne({ 'local.email' :  email },
      function(err, user) {
        // if errors
        if (err) {
          return done(err);
        }
      // check email
      if (user) {
        return done(null, false,
        req.flash('signupMessage','Warning! the email is
        already taken.'));
      } else {
        // create the user
        var newUser = new User();
        newUser.local.email = email;
        newUser.local.password =
          newUser.generateHash(password);
        newUser.save(function(err) {
          if (err) {
            throw err;
          }
```

```
                return done(null, newUser);
            });
        }
    });
    } else {
        // everything ok, register user
        return done(null, req.user);
    }
    });
    }));
};
```

We wrote a basic configuration for using Passport. You can find more information regarding this process at `http://passportjs.org/guide/configure/` and `http://passportjs.org/guide/username-password/`.

Note that we implemented a warning message using the `connect-flash` module. This is a simple module to show warning messages to a user. The flash messages are stored in the session.

Using this module, we can easily show messages just using the `req.flash()` function, as we used in the previous code, by following these steps:

1. Open your terminal and type the following command:

    npm install connect-flash --save

2. Place the flash module into the `server.js` file after the Mongoose variable with the following code:

    ```
    var flash = require('connect-flash');
    ```

3. Add the following highlighted code to the `app.use()` function:

    ```
    ....
    app.use('/api/speakers', speakers);
    // flash warning messages
    app.use(flash());
    ```

4. We have flash messages that are ready to use. To finish the Passport configuration, we need to import the Passport module and add to the `app.use()` function in the `server.js` file.

5. Add the following code to the `server.js` file, after the `flash` variable:

    ```
    var flash = require('connect-flash');
    var passport = require('passport');
    ```

6. Add the following highlighted code to the `app.use()` function:

```
// flash warning messages
app.use(flash());
// Init passport authentication
app.use(passport.initialize());
// persistent login sessions
app.use(passport.session());
```

After performing these steps, we now have the baseline to use Passport, but we still need to perform some more steps. Let's go ahead and add session control and password encryption.

Adding session control and password encryption

To take care of adding session control and password encryption, two important tasks, we will use two very useful middleware: `express-session`, which as the name suggests controls the user session, and `connect-mongo` to store the user session on MongoDB.

1. Open your terminal and type the following command:

   ```
   npm install express-session connect-mongo --save
   ```

2. Add the module to the `server.js` file with the following highlighted code:

   ```
   var passport = require('passport');
   // Modules to store session
   var session = require('express-session');
   var MongoStore = require('connect-mongo')(session);
   ```

3. Add the following highlighted code to the `app.use()` function:

   ```
   app.use(passport.session());
   // required for passport
   // secret for session
   app.use(session({
     secret: 'sometextgohere',
     saveUninitialized: true,
     resave: true,
     //store session on MongoDB using express-session + connect
     mongo
     store: new MongoStore({
       url: config.url,
       collection : 'sessions'
       })
   }));
   ```

Note that, besides using the session, here we determined that MongoDB stores the user session in a collection called sessions.

 You can find more information about `express-session` at `https://github.com/expressjs/session`.

4. Now, let's add the `bcrypt-nodejs` module to deal with password encryption. The first step is to install the module. Open your terminal and type:

```
npm install bcrypt-nodejs --save
```

Password encryption is a security measure widely adopted in web applications, and the Node.js ecosystem gives us this great alternative.

You can find more about `bcrypt` for Node.js applications at `https://github.com/shaneGirish/bcrypt-nodejs`.

In the next section, we'll see how to use this middleware on a user model.

Setting password encryption to a user model

Let's continue to use the `bcrypt` module and implement it in our user model.

First, let's create the file where we will use this module. Do not yet perform any change in the `server.js` file as we did previously with other modules; this is due to the fact that we will use it only in the user model.

1. Add a new file called `user.js` to the `models` folder.

2. Now, let's create a Mongoose schema to hold the user password and e-mail. Place the following code in the `user.js` file:

```
// Import mongoose and bcrypt
var mongoose = require('mongoose');
var bcrypt = require('bcrypt-nodejs');

var Schema = mongoose.Schema;

// define the schema for our user model
var userSchema = new Schema({

  local: {
  email: String,
  password: String,
  }
```

```
        });

    // generating a hash
    userSchema.methods.generateHash = function(password) {
      return bcrypt.hashSync(password, bcrypt.genSaltSync(8), null);
    };

    // validating if password is valid
    userSchema.methods.validPassword = function(password) {
      return bcrypt.compareSync(password, this.local.password);
    };

    // create the model for users and export to app
    module.exports = mongoose.model('User', userSchema);
```

Note that we use `bcrypt` to generate a hash for the password in the highlighted code and also a validate method (`methods.validPassword`) to check whether the password is valid.

Reviewing the changes in the server.js file

It's time to revise all changes made in the `server.js` file, just to check whether something is missing. The highlighted lines of code indicate that they were added in this stage.

Your file should look like the following code:

```
// Import the Modules / assign modules to variables
var express = require('express');
var path = require('path');
var favicon = require('static-favicon');
var logger = require('morgan');
var cookieParser = require('cookie-parser');
var bodyParser = require('body-parser');
var mongoose = require('mongoose');
var flash = require('connect-flash');
var passport = require('passport');

// Modules to store session
var session = require('express-session');
var MongoStore = require('connect-mongo')(session);

// Setup Routes
var routes = require('./server/routes/index');
var users = require('./server/routes/users');
```

```
var speakers = require('./server/routes/speakers');

// Database configuration
var config = require('./server/config/config.js');
// connect to our database
mongoose.connect(config.url);
// Check if MongoDB is running
mongoose.connection.on('error', function() {
  console.error('MongoDB Connection Error. Make sure MongoDB is
  running.');
});

var app = express();

// Passport configuration
require('./server/config/passport')(passport);

// view engine setup
app.set('views', path.join(__dirname, 'server/views'));
app.set('view engine', 'ejs');

app.use(favicon());
app.use(logger('dev'));
app.use(bodyParser.json());
app.use(bodyParser.urlencoded());
app.use(cookieParser());
app.use(express.static(path.join(__dirname, 'public')));

// required for passport
// secret for session
app.use(session({
  secret: 'sometextgohere',
  saveUninitialized: true,
  resave: true,
  //store session on MongoDB using express-session + connect mongo
  store: new MongoStore({
    url: config.url,
    collection : 'sessions'
    })
}));

// flash warning messages
app.use(flash());
// Init passport authentication
```

```
app.use(passport.initialize());
// persistent login sessions
app.use(passport.session());

// using routes
app.use('/', routes);
app.use('/users', users);
app.use('/api/speakers', speakers);

// catch 404 and forward to error handler
app.use(function(req, res, next) {
  var err = new Error('Not Found');
  err.status = 404;
  next(err);
});

// error handlers

// development error handler
// will print stacktrace
if (app.get('env') == 'development') {
  app.use(function(err, req, res, next) {
    res.status(err.status || 500);
    res.render('error', {
      message: err.message,
      error: err
    });
  });
}

// production error handler
// no stacktraces leaked to user
app.use(function(err, req, res, next) {
  res.status(err.status || 500);
  res.render('error', {
    message: err.message,
    error: {}
  });
});

module.exports = app;
```

```
app.set('port', process.env.PORT || 3000);

var server = app.listen(app.get('port'), function() {
  console.log('Express server listening on port ' +
  server.address().port);
});
```

Dealing with routes

Now that we have completed the implementation of user authentication, we need to configure the application routes to handle the validation and creation of users.

Let's make some changes in the `index.js` file inside the `routes` folder:

1. Add the following highlighted code to the `index.js` file:

```
var express = require('express');
var router = express.Router();
var passport = require('passport');

/* GET home page. */
router.get('/', function(req, res) {
  res.render('index.ejs');
});

module.exports = router;
```

Note that we set up the default router to render a page called `index.ejs`. We have not created this page yet, but we will do so soon; for now, we will continue setting the necessary routes to handle authentication.

2. Let's create the route for a `profile.ejs` page; place the following code after the `home page` route function:

```
/* GET profile page. */
router.get('/profile', isLoggedIn, function(req, res) {
  res.render('profile.ejs', {
    user : req.user
  });
});
```

Here, we passed an `isLoggedIn` function as a parameter of the `router.get()` function and a user object as the second parameter for the `res.render()` function. This indicates that the user must be logged in to see this page.

3. So, the next step is to create the `isLoggedIn()` function. Add the following lines of code after the `profile` route:

```
// function to check if user is logged in
function isLoggedIn(req, res, next) {
  if (req.isAuthenticated()) {
    return next();
  }
  // if not logged go to default route
  res.redirect('/');
}
```

Now, we need to deal with logging out of the application; instead of creating a function, we will create a route to perform this action. So, any time we access the `/logout` route, we end the user session.

4. Add the following code right after the profile route:

```
/* GET logout route. */
router.get('/logout', function(req, res) {
  req.logout();
  res.redirect('/');
});
```

We still need two more routes: one for the login page and another for the signup page; these routes will have two routes functions: one for the GET method and the other for the POST method.

5. Add the following code after the `profile` route:

```
/* GET login page. */
router.get('/login', function(req, res) {
  res.render('login.ejs', { message:
    req.flash('loginMessage') });
});
```

```
/* POST login data. */
router.post('/login', passport.authenticate('local-login', {
  //Success go to Profile Page / Fail go to login page
  successRedirect : '/profile',
  failureRedirect : '/login',
  failureFlash : true
}));
```

6. Add the following code after the `login` route:

```
/* GET signup page. */
router.get('/signup', function(req, res) {
  res.render('signup.ejs', { message: req.flash('signupMessage')
});
});

/* POST signup data. */
router.post('/signup', passport.authenticate('local-signup', {
  //Success go to Profile Page / Fail go to Signup page
  successRedirect : '/profile',
  failureRedirect : '/signup',
  failureFlash : true
}));
```

Note that we are passing a flash message as the second parameter of the `res.
render()` function with a warning message from the `passport.js` file. Also, we
use the Passport methods `successRedirect`, `failureRedirect`, and `failureFlash`
to deal with success and fail, redirecting to a specific page and sending warning
messages if the session fails.

Now, we need to create the pages for each previous function, so we will
use templates.

Templates with Embedded JavaScript

At the beginning of the chapter, we adopted the mechanism of templates called
EJS, which is very easy to understand. Besides, EJS gives us the template logic
functionality within its syntax and can be easily embedded within HTML files.
Its use is very similar to that of Handlebars, another excellent JavaScript library
to use templates; for example:

```
<h1><%= title %></h1>
<ul>
  <% for( var i = 0; i < bands.length; i++ ) { %>
    <li>
      <%= bands[i] %>
    </li>
  <% } %>
</ul>
```

It is very similar to other programming languages such as PHP and RoR.

However, you can use the template that suits you; Node.js has a great list of template engines for all tastes.

 Another good option for a template engine is Swig, which can be installed through the npm command:

`npm install swig`

1. Let's create the following files' templates in the `views` folder:

   ○ `login.ejs`

   ○ `profile.ejs`

   ○ `signup.ejs`

2. Also, we will create a folder called `common` inside the `views` folder to store some common files between the pages, using the `include` functionality from the EJS template engine.

3. In the `common` folder, add two files called `head.ejs` and `footer.ejs`. Now we have the necessary files and our application structure inside the `server` folder should look like the following screenshot:

Later in this chapter, we will add content to EJS templates; for now, let's use a very useful tool called the Bower dependency manager.

Bower leading frontend dependencies

Bower will take care of all of our frontend dependencies. Of course, it is simpler to just add the CSS and image files directly in the `public` folder, but we need a scalable application, right? There is nothing better than using Bower to manage frontend dependencies. To install the dependencies, we will perform the following steps:

1. Go to the `root` folder and create a new file named `bower.json`.

2. Create another file named `.bowerrc` with the following code:

```
{
    "directory": "public/bower_components"
}
```

   The behavior of `bower.json` is very similar to `package.json` and both use the `init` command to create the package file. We skip this step, and add our dependencies directly into the file.

3. Place the following code in the `bower.json` file:

```
{
    "name": "conference-api",
    "version": "0.0.1",
    "dependencies": {
        "purecss": "~0.5.0"
    }
}
```

4. Open your terminal and type the following command:

```
bower install
```

As we can see, we will be using the Pure CSS framework to handle our frontend code inside our templates.

1. If you open the `public` folder, inside the application root, you can see the `bower_components` folder created with our Pure CSS package. You can name the directory as you like. For this example, the name `bower_components` is very appropriate, as shown in the following screenshot:

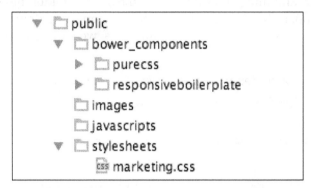

2. Now, we'll install the Responsive Boilerplate grid system. Open your terminal and type the following command:

```
bower install responsiveboilerplate#2.3.2 --save
```

Note that command will install a specific version of the framework and then save the dependency in our `bower.json` file.

Pure CSS and Responsive Boilerplate for frontend views

As we have seen in the previous chapter, we use Pure CSS and Responsive Boilerplate in our frontend to style the appearance of our templates.

As we do not need any more introductions to these tools, we will directly perform the implementation of the layout. For this example application, we will use a readymade layout that can be downloaded for free from `http://purecss.io/layouts/`. We will use the Landing Page layout example with minor changes, just so that it fits exactly to our needs for the conference website. After downloading the layout, perform the following steps:

1. First of all, copy the `marketing.css` file from the `layout` folder inside the `css` folder from your downloaded package.

2. Place the `marketing.css` stylesheet in the `stylesheets` folder inside the `public` directory.

Creating the index, profile, login, and signup pages

In this section, we will add the necessary HTML content to format the style of the templates stored in the `views` folder in the `server` directory. Before we start, let's edit `head.ejs` and `footer.ejs`. We use the `<% include %>` functionality to keep the header and footer of all templates in one place. To create the index, profile, login, and signup pages perform the following steps:

1. Add the following content to the `head.ejs` template:

```
<head>
  <title>Conference API</title>
  <link rel="stylesheet"
  href="//netdna.bootstrapcdn.com/font-awesome/4.0.3/css/font-
awesome.min.css">
  <link rel="stylesheet"
href="/bower_components/responsiveboilerplate/css/responsiv
eboilerplate.min.css">
  <link rel="stylesheet"
href="/bower_components/purecss/src/base/css/base.css">
  <link rel="stylesheet"
href="/bower_components/purecss/src/buttons/css/buttons.css
">
  <link rel="stylesheet"
href="/bower_components/purecss/src/buttons/css/buttons-core.css">
  <link rel="stylesheet"
href="/bower_components/purecss/src/forms/css/forms.css">
  <link rel="stylesheet"
href="/bower_components/purecss/src/menus/css/menus.css">
  <link rel="stylesheet"
href="/bower_components/purecss/src/menus/css/menus-core.css">
  <link rel="stylesheet"
href="/stylesheets/marketing.css">
  <style>
    .container {
      width: 60%;
      margin: 0 auto;
      padding-top: 80px;
    }
    .alert {
      color: #fff;
```

```
        padding: 10px;
        background-color: #ff0000;
      }
    </style>
  </head>
```

2. Add the following content to the `footer.ejs` template:

```
<div class="content-wrapper">
  <div class="footer l-box is-center">
    Conference-API @ 2014
  </div>
</div>
```

3. Open the `index.js` file and place the following code:

```
<!doctype html>
<html>
<% include common/head %>
<body>
<div class="header">
  <div class="home-menu pure-menu pure-menu-open pure-menu-
horizontal pure-menu-fixed">
    <a class="pure-menu-heading" href="">Conference API</a>
    <ul>
      <li class="pure-menu-selected"><a href="/">
Home</a></li>
        <li><a href="/login"> Login</a></li>
        <li><a href="/signup"> Signup</a></li>
      </ul>
    </div>
</div>

<div class="splash-container">
  <div class="splash">
    <h1 class="splash-head">Conference</h1>
    <p class="splash-subhead">
      Lorem ipsum dolor sit amet, consectetur adipisicing
      elit.
    </p>
    <p>
      <a href="/login" class="pure-button pure-button-
primary">View Speakers</a>
    </p>
  </div>
</div>
```

```
<% include common/footer %>
</body>
</html>
```

We made some changes in the original index file from the Pure CSS layout template just to fit our needs:

1. Removed some unnecessary blocks of code from our example.
2. Removed some style rules for IE 8.
3. Added the Responsive Boilerplate grid system.
4. Added Pure CSS as separate styles form base, buttons, forms, and menus.

4. At this stage, when you run the command, `node server`, you will see the home page at `http://localhost:3000/`, as shown in the following screenshot:

5. Open the `login.ejs` file and place the following content:

```
<!doctype html>
<html>
<% include common/head %>
<body>
<div class="header">
  <div class="home-menu pure-menu pure-menu-open pure-menu-
horizontal pure-menu-fixed">
    <a class="pure-menu-heading" href="">Conference API</a>
    <ul>
```

```
            <li><a href="/"> Home</a></li>
            <li class="pure-menu-selected"><a href="/login">
            Login</a></li>
            <li><a href="/signup"> Signup</a></li>
          </ul>
      </div>
    </div>
    <div class="container">
      <h1> Login</h1>
      <% if (message.length > 0) { %>
        <div class="alert"><%= message %></div>
      <% } %>
      <form action="/login" method="post" class="pure-form">
        <fieldset>
          <input id="email" class="pure-input-1" type="email"
            placeholder="Email Address" name="email" required>
          <input id="password" class="pure-input-1"
            type="password" placeholder="Password"
            name="password" required>
          <button type="submit" class="pure-button pure-button-
primary">Submit</button>
          <p>Don't have an account?
            <a href="/signup">Signup</a> or go back to
            <a href="/">home</a>.</p>
        </fieldset>
      </form>
    </div>
    <% include common/footer %>
  </body>
</html>
```

Note that here we use the logic of our EJS template engine with `<% if () %>` to show a warning message if our login credentials fail. Also, the `style` tag in the document `head` is used to style the messages.

Here is the result of our login page:

6. Open the `signup.ejs` file and place the following content:

```
<!doctype html>
<html>
<% include common/head %>
<body>
<div class="header">
   <div class="home-menu pure-menu pure-menu-open pure-menu-
horizontal pure-menu-fixed">
      <a class="pure-menu-heading" href="">Conference API</a>
      <ul>
         <li><a href="/">Home</a></li>
         <li><a href="/login"> Login</a></li>
         <li class="pure-menu-selected"><a href="/signup">
            Signup</a></li>
      </ul>
   </div>
</div>
<div class="container">
   <h1> Signup</h1>
   <% if (message.length > 0) { %>
      <div class="alert"><%= message %></div>
   <% } %>
   <form action="/signup" method="post" class="pure-form">
      <fieldset>
         <input id="email" class="pure-input-1" type="email"
            placeholder="Email Address" name="email" required>
         <input id="password" class="pure-input-1"
            type="password" placeholder="Password"
            name="password" required>
         <button type="submit" class="pure-button pure-button-
primary">Submit</button>
         <p>Have an account? <a href="/login">Login</a> or go
            back to <a href="/">home</a>.</p>
      </fieldset>
   </form>
</div>
<% include common/footer %>
</body>
</html>
```

7. Check the browser at `http://localhost:3000/signup` and you will see the following:

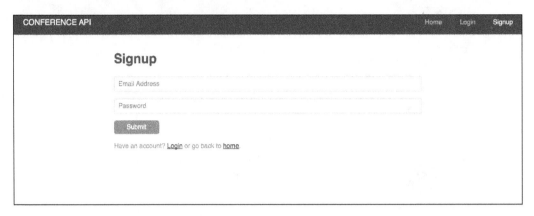

8. Now the final step for our templates; let's perform the same process to create the profile page. Open `profile.ejs` and place the following content:

```
<!doctype html>
<html>
<% include common/head %>
<body>
<div class="header">
  <div class="home-menu pure-menu pure-menu-open pure-menu-
horizontal pure-menu-fixed">
    <a class="pure-menu-heading" href="">Conference API</a>
    <ul>
      <li><a href="/profile"><span class="fa fa-
user"></span> <%= user.local.email %></a></li>
      <li><a href="/logout" class="btn btn-default">
        <span class="fa fa-power-off"></span>
        Logout</a></li>
    </ul>
  </div>
</div>
<div class="container">
  <div class="datails">
    <h3><span class="fa fa-user"></span> User Details</h3>
    <p> Welcome - <strong>email</strong>:
      <%= user.local.email %><br>
    </p>
  </div>
</div>
<% include common/footer %>
</body>
</html>
```

We added the user e-mail address link and the logout link, so when you click on **Logout,** our /logout route will redirect us to the index page.

Here, we again use the EJS template language to show the user info, which in this case is only the e-mail address, as shown in the following screenshot:

Finally our building process is finished. Now let's commit our work to Git and prepare for the next chapters.

 Git is an open source tool to source control; you can find more information at http://git-scm.com/.

Summary

We reached the end of another chapter; this was a real journey into the heart of development using the Express framework through the implementation of authenticating users with Passport, sessions, and the encryption of passwords.

We also saw how to use the Bower dependency manager and refactor an application generated with the Express generator, making its structure optimized to eventually be able to scale our application without major hassle. However, we still have much to look forward to. In the next chapter, we will begin our frontend development with AngularJS and tools such as Yeoman and Grunt.js.

5
Starting with AngularJS

Although it is easy to start developing SPAs with AngularJS, but over time and as your application grows, there will be tasks that are more difficult to solve. So, it is very important to understand all the concepts very well. Unlike other JavaScript frameworks, AngularJS adopts a more connected approach to the HTML syntax, functioning as a kind of language extension.

We consider these topics as core concepts for a good understanding of the AngularJS framework: directives, scope, services, controllers, dependency injection, and expressions. Even this seems a lot, but it is not if we take into account the complexity of the framework. However, as this book is not an absolute guide to AngularJS, we will only discuss here a few concepts that are considered as fundamentals to build SPAs. Once the concepts are understood, you will have the necessary basics to move forward with the framework.

Throughout this chapter, we will be focusing on the following concepts:

- Starting the baseline application
- The AngularJS MVC pattern implementation
  - Model
  - View
  - Controller
- Detailing directives, expressions, and scope
- Two-way data binding and templates
- Understanding dependency injection
- Services
- Modules
- Project organization
- Pattern implementation

As we said, AngularJS is a powerful tool to develop SPAs and can also be considered as an MVC or MVVM framework; its flexibility is so great that it suits our needs. Let's understand some concepts to help us to choose the better way.

Starting the baseline application

As with any web application, we kick off with creating a basic page. Later, we will discuss all the components that appear in the following example, but this time, we focus on the basic initialization of an AngularJS application:

```
<html ng-app>
  <head>
    <title>Angular baseline</title>
    <script
src="https://cdnjs.cloudflare.com/ajax/libs/angular.js/1.2.20/angu
lar.min.js"></script>
  </head>
  <body>
    <input type="text" ng-model="name">
    <p>Hello: {{ name }}</p>
  </body>
</html>
```

By declaring the `ng-app` property on the `html` tag, we are initializing our application. It's the first of some new properties that we will use. The entire framework revolves around these new statements.

The `ng-app` property informs that our **Document Object Model (DOM)** and HTML document are also an AngularJS document. This property can be used in any element of the DOM. In many cases, only a single part of the HTML will be an AngularJS application, as shown in the following example:

```
<html>
  <head>
    <title>Angular baseline</title>
    <script
src="https://cdnjs.cloudflare.com/ajax/libs/angular.js/1.2.20/angu
lar.min.js"></script>
  </head>
  <body>
    <div id="main">
      <div class="container">
        <div id="main-app" ng-app="myAngularApp">
          <!--Application content will be rendered here-->
        </div>
```

```
      </div>
    </div>
    <script src="path_to_JavaScript_files"></script>
  </body>
</html>
```

Finally, the JavaScript files that are part of the project are added to the end of the HTML page like the previous example. In a real application, these files will be models, controllers, directives, and everything related to the application.

The AngularJS MVC pattern implementation

AngularJS follows the MVC pattern of software engineering and encourages loose coupling between presentation, data, and logic components. However, in the AngularJS framework, we do not declare the model as in other MVC libraries such as Ember.js and Backbone.js.

In AngularJS, we declare the model within the controller, through the use of $scope. Let's check the MVC behavior inside AngularJS in the upcoming sections.

Model

AngularJS Model can be considered as a JavaScript object or a primitive JavaScript type such as string, number, boolean, or complex objects.

Synthesizing its definition, AngularJS Model is a JavaScript object inside controllers using $scope. The properties and behaviors that represent the object can be accessed by its respective View.

Later, we will go deeper in to the use of $scope; for now, let's see a simple example:

```
function UserController($scope) {
  // A simple JavaScript object to hold our Model
  var user;

  user = {
    // User properties, add as many as you need
    name: "Fernando",
    age: "25"
  }

  $scope.user = user
}
```

The preceding snippet is based on pure JavaScript object and is assigned to `$scope.user`, we can declare it directly as:

```
function UserController($scope) {
  $scope.user = {
    // User properties, add as many as you need
    name: "Fernando",
    age: "25"
  }
}
```

There are several ways to declare objects within the controller, and you can choose the way that suits you.

View

Imagine that View is what we have in the browser; it is where the user interacts with our application, manipulating DOM. This is done using AngularJS expressions. Expressions are a very practical way to interact with the View (HTML) example:

```
<div ng-controller="UserController">
  <h1>{{ user.name }}</h1>
</div>
```

Its syntax is comprised of double brackets and the name of the variable / property that we want to render. There is another way to do the same, using `ng-bind`:

```
<div ng-controller="UserController">
  <h1 ng-bind="user.name"></h1>
</div>
```

The main difference is if AngularJS takes a while to compile the application code, the user might see the double brackets expression before the content. To avoid this type of behavior, we can use the `ng-cloak` directive, applied to the body element on the HTML page, as shown in the following code:

```
<body ng-cloak>
```

Otherwise, we can use the `ng-cloak` directive inside any HTML element of the page as follows:

```
<div ng-controller="BandController" ng-cloak>
  <ul>
    <li ng-repeat="band in bands">{{ band.name }} - {{ band.album
    }}</li>
  </ul>
</div>
```

By the use of two-way data binding of AngularJS, this expression is bound to the property of our Controller to server.

Controller

Taking into consideration the definition of Controller in the MVC pattern, Controller is where we place all the application logic. However, in AngularJS, controllers are like classes in JavaScript, and here is where our AngularJS Model resides, as we mentioned earlier.

The AngularJS controller concept is quite different from other MVC libraries, where we can create models separately from controllers' code, like in Backbone.js and Ember.js.

Let's take a look at how it all relates. For the following example, we use all the JavaScript code in the same file, but for a modular and scalable development, you must organize each file in its place:

```html
<html>
<head>
  <title>Angular MVC Example</title>
</head>
<!-- Setup Angular App -->
<body ng-app>
  <!-- Setup User Controller -->
  <div ng-controller="UserController">
    <h1>{{ user.name }} - {{ user.age }}</h1>
  </div>
  <!-- Setup Band Controler -->
  <div ng-controller="BandController">
    <ul>
      <li ng-repeat="band in bands">{{ band.name }} - {{
      band.album }}</li>
    </ul>
  </div>
  <!-- Include Angular -->
  <script src="https://ajax.googleapis.com/ajax/libs/angularjs/1.2.20/
angular.min.js"></script>
  <script>
    // Set the controller with a basic function
    function UserController($scope) {
      // A simple JavaScript object to hold our Model
      var user;
      user = {
```

```
        // User properties, add as many as you need
        name: "Fernando",
        age: "25"
      }

    $scope.user = user
  }

  function BandController($scope) {
    // A simple JavaScript object to hold our Model
    // using $scope
    $scope.bands = [
    {name: "Metallica", album: "Master of Puppets" },
    {name: "Slayer", album: "Seasons in the Abyss"},
    {name: "Anthrax", album: "Persistence of Time"}
    ];
  }
}
</script>
</body>
</html>
```

In this simple example, we can see something beyond what we talked about previously: ng-app, ng-controller, and ng-repeat.

Now, we'll see what this means in more detail.

Detailing directives, expressions, and scope

The first thing we notice when we look at the previous example is the presence of the np-app tag; this is known as directives, and in this specific example, it serves to tell AngularJS that all code contained within the body tag is an AngularJS application, as we mentioned before.

After this, we have ng-controller; as the name mentions, here we declare which controller will act on a certain region of HTML, and ng-repeat is something like a built-in loop over arrays. For simplicity, the tags, ng-app, ng-controller, and ng-repeat, are the AngularJS directives; there are many others as well.

To simplify, ng-atributtes (such as ng-app, ng-bind, ng-show, and ng-hide) are built-in directives of the framework; we can also create custom directives.

More information about Angular directives can be found at `https://docs.angularjs.org/api/ng/directive`.

Directives serve to extend the grammar of HTML and are simple statements but have powerful and flexible features. In addition to the existing directives, we can create four types of directives:

- Element directives
- Attribute directives
- CSS class directives
- Comment directives

The following are the four ways to create a custom directive:

Restrict	Markup
'A'	`<span ng-directivename></span>`
'E'	`<ng-directivename></ng-directivename>`
'C'	`<span class="ng-directivename"></span>`
'M'	`<!-- directive: ng- directivename-->`

The base code for a custom directive is as follows:

```
app.directive('ngDirectivename', function() {
  return {
    restrict: 'A',
    // Doing your Directive code here
  }
});
```

Note that we created an element directive with the keyword `'A'` and invoke/use it in HTML as follows:

```
<div ng-Directivename></div>
```

Here's an example in practice, a basic element directive:

```
myAngularApp = angular.module("myAngularApp", []);

myAngularApp.directive('div', function() {
  var directive = {};

  // Restrict directive to html elements
```

```
    directive.restrict = 'E';

    // Set a basic template
    directive.template = "My Angular directive: {{ someTextGoesHere
    }}";

    return directive;
});
```

The first parameter to the `directive()` function is the directive name. This name will use the HTML template to activate the directive. The second parameter passed to the `directive()` function is a factory function. This function returns the directive definition when invoked.

The `directive.template` property will replace the {{ someTextGoesHere }} expression for the controller property, $scope.someTextGoesHere, as shown in the following example:

```
<div ng-controller="MyAngularController" >
  <directivename >This will be replaced for the Controllers $scope
  content</directivename>
</div>

<script>
  myAngularApp = angular.module("myAngularApp", []);
  // Creating the Directive
  myAngularApp.directive('directivename', function() {
    var directive = {};

    // Applying only to HTML elements
    directive.restrict = 'E';

    // Set a basic template
    directive.template = "My Angular directive: {{
    someTextGoesHere }}";

    return directive;
  });

  // Setup a Controller
  myAngularApp.controller("MyAngularController", function($scope)
  {
    $scope.someTextGoesHere = "My first Directive is working";

  });
</script>
```

Finally, when the code is rendered, we will have the **My first Directive is working** string.

As mentioned before, the double brackets in {{ `someTextGoesHere` }} are AngularJS expressions, and finally in our `MyAngularController` directive, we can see the scope again.

`$scope` is a kind of link between Controller and View, and each controller has its own scope. Note that we used `$scope` in two ways: directly in the variable, as we saw in the previous example, and assigning to a variable. The most common way is `$scope.name = {}`. Here is a diagram to illustrate the Angular diagram of scope:

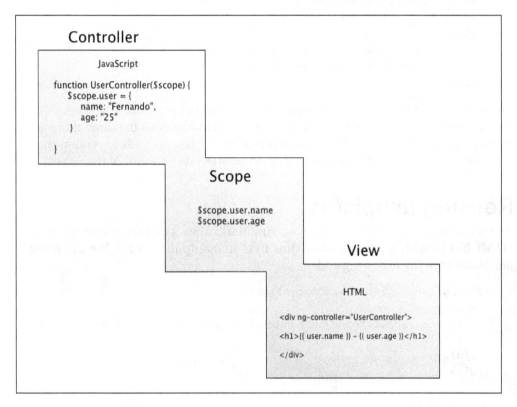

In the preceding figure, we note that the behavior of `$scope` interacts between the Controller and the View, acting like a ViewModel.

Two-way data binding and templates

Two-way data binding is one of the most interesting parts of AngularJS. It is responsible for synchronizing changes made to Model, and it manipulates DOM instantly. Without their help, it would need to write many, many lines of code to monitor changes to Model and return them to update DOM.

Let's see the following code, which illustrates the data binding:

```
<div ng-controller="UserController">
  <h1>{{ user.name }} - {{ user.age }}</h1>
  <p ng-bind="user.name"></p>
  <p ng-bind="user.age"></p>
  <br>
  <input type="text" ng-model="user.name">
  <input type="text" ng-model="user.age">
</div>
```

Just below the `<h1>` tag, where we used the expression with double brackets, we can see two paragraphs with the `ng-bind` directive; it does the same thing as the expression, but if the code for some reason take a few seconds to render, the user can view the double brackets before AngularJS takes control of the page.

Reusing templates

As we can see in the previous example, AngularJS allows us to create templates; HTML blocks with expressions and directives to manipulate DOM. We can reuse templates with the following code:

```
<div ng-controller="BandController">
  <ul>
    <li ng-repeat="band in bands">{{ band.name }} - {{ band.album
    }}</li>
  </ul>
</div>
```

Understanding dependency injection

Dependency injection is a common software design pattern and widely used in AngularJS; it is similar to what we have in the Express framework using `require()`. You just need to add the services as parameters to controllers, directives, or functions. Many of these items will depend on others to work. For example, a controller request to the server will need the `$http` service, and this service has to come from somewhere.

To facilitate this configuration, AngularJS provides three ways to declare dependencies:

- Directly using the parameters of a function, as we can see in the following example:

```
function UserController($scope, $http, $resource,
$ownservice) {
  var user;

  $scope.user = {
    name: "Fernando",
    age: "25"
  }
}
```

- Using an array, as shown here:

```
User.controller ('UserController', ['$scope','$http' function
($scope, $http) {...}]);
```

- Using the $inject property, as follows:

```
UserController var = function ($scope, $http) {...};
UserController $ inject = ['$scope','$http'].;
user.Module.controller ('UserController' UserController);
```

> The best way is to use an array, which in the case of file compression/minify, prevents possible function damage due to character replacement of variable names.
>
> You can find more about dependency injection in Angular at https://github.com/angular/angular.js/wiki/Understanding-Dependency-Injection.

Services

Services are often interpreted incorrectly. They can be easily confused with Ajax requests that are used with some backend service via the HTTP protocol. However, services are singleton, a function, or an object and can be used to hold and share data, through controllers, directives, filters, and other services. Also, you are free to create your own services; just register the service's name and the service factory function, with an Angular module. The service factory function creates the object or function and exposes the service to the rest of the AngularJS application.

```
var userModule = angular.module('userModule', []);
userModule.factory('server', function() {
```

```
    var serverServiceInstance;
    ...
    return serverServiceInstance;
});
```

A `.service()` and `.factory()` function always have a `return` statement. Being singleton had only one instance of a specific service per injector available in the entire life of the AngularJS application. Other services are constant, value, and provider; more about services can be found on the official documentation at `https://docs.angularjs.org/guide/services`.

Modules in AngularJS

In AngularJS, modules are structured to build highly scalable web applications. We can create them and use them throughout the application.

It is very simple to create and inject it in the application. From the AngularJS documentation, they define modules as:

> Modules are a container for the different parts of your app such as controllers, services, filters, directives, and so on.
>
> More details about modules, can be found at `https://docs.angularjs.org/api/ng/type/angular.Module`.

Modules can contain a collection of other components/dependencies such as controllers, services, directives, and others.

The basic simple form to create a module is as follows:

```
angular.module(ModuleName, [requires dependency]);
```

The basic simple form to use a module is as follows:

```
angular.module('ModuleName');
```

Let's see a practical way to declare and instantiate a module and Controller:

```
angular.module(User, ['$scope']);

angular.module('User')
.run(function($scope) {
  $scope.user = { name: 'Fernando' }
});
angular.module('User').controller('UserController', function () {
  //Controller content here
});
```

This way, we can add as many modules as necessary to our application:

```
angular.module('User', ['$scope']);
angular.module("Message", ['$scope', '$User']);
angular.module("Deliver", ['Deliver']);
angular.module("Mailbox", ['Inbox', 'Compose']);
```

Project organization

Now, we enter a very controversial subject when it comes to applications with AngularJS. There are many ways to configure your environment for development using the framework. Interpret how to configure the environment and structure the directories in a way that allows us to scale it with ease.

Probably, if you make a brief search, you will find many ways to do this; this is totally acceptable, but for sure, you will find your own way to do it. Until then, we will present some alternatives.

The official AngularJS project has a simple boilerplate to start angular-seed; you can find it at https://github.com/angular/angular-seed.

The following screenshot shows angular-seed's structure:

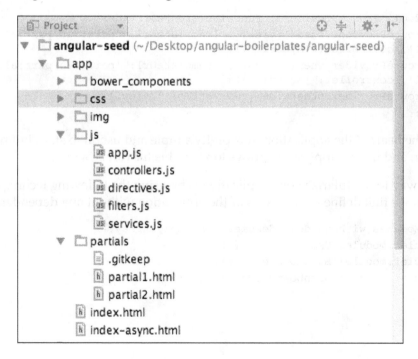

Generally, the whole structure of AngularJS applications are structured in a directory called App, and there are many ways of using this directory. For now, imagine that the application is growing over time and you need to add more controllers in a single file called controllers.js and the same for services, directives, and filters quickly; you will surely be in trouble.

Not to mention keeping all controllers of an application in a single file, does not make your team productive.

Switching back to angular-seed, the most important file here and in almost all AngularJS applications is app.js, which is an alias to application.js. Let's see its content:

```
'use strict';

// Declare app level module which depends on filters, and services
angular.module('myApp', [
  'ngRoute',
  'myApp.filters',
  'myApp.services',
  'myApp.directives',
  'myApp.controllers'
]).
config(['$routeProvider', function($routeProvider) {
  $routeProvider.when('/view1', {templateUrl: 'partials/partial1.
html', controller: 'MyCtrl1'});
  $routeProvider.when('/view2', {templateUrl: 'partials/partial2.
html', controller: 'MyCtrl2'});
  $routeProvider.otherwise({redirectTo: '/view1'});
}]);
```

Here's the heart of the application. It is pretty simple and useful to start, but not very modular, and if your application grows too big, this file can be a mess.

A good way to modularize your application is by using the following technique; note that we first define the modules of the application without any dependency:

```
// Modules without dependencies, an empty Array.
angular.module('UserModule', []);
angular.module('BandModule', []);
angular.module('DashboardModule', []);
```

```
angular.module('LoginModule', []);
// A main module with all modules as dependencies
angular.module('MainApp',
    [
        'UserModule',
        'BandModule',
        'DashboardApp',
        'LoginModule',
    ]
);
```

Then, we define a main module and place all the preceding modules as dependencies. Anyway, it's still highly recommended from the starting point; it also has a dedicated test directory, one folder for testing **end to end (e2e)**, and another one for unit tests.

Testing is another key point of the structure of the framework; AngularJS was designed with testing in mind. This is another point that makes AngularJS an unbelievably productive tool. There are countless testing frameworks, which serve several purposes such as unit testing and TDD tests among others.

Nowadays, it is very important that you test your code; it also means that the more tests you write, the less the chances of your job failing at the end of a long journey of development.

> We recommend Karma for AngularJS testing. Karma is a well-known testing framework and works very well with AngularJS applications. To know more about Karma, check out http://karma-runner.github.io/0.12/index.html.
>
> Also, Karma (known before as Testacular) had a very easy integration with the Webstorm IDE.

But how we can be more modular with AngularJS?

Let's take a look at the following example; we note that the modules are each in their directory. Including submodules belonging to a module in the case of the user's account.

Here, we have the login modules, configurations, and signup within a directory named `account`:

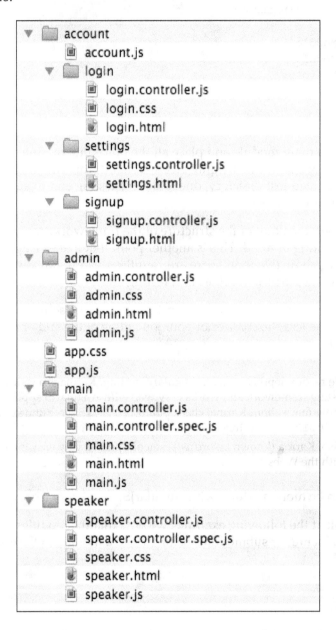

Everything is modular, including the CSS files and the test files. Every folder is a module with all related files together in one place. In the next chapter, we will discuss more about this structure.

Summary

We have finally exhausted one more chapter. In this chapter, we describe the key concepts of the utilization of AngularJS.

We have followed the key items to gain a good understanding on the use of the framework.

As mentioned earlier, we quoted only the concepts that are relevant to the example application we are building throughout our book.

For more details, we strongly recommend reading all the official AngularJS documentation. If you still have some query, you can quickly find the answer there.

In the next chapter, we will see how to use AngularJS in the frontend of our application; we will go through all the topics covered in this chapter and will see some things we have not discussed so far. We will go through some common problems with authentication and permissions between the views, routes, and some very useful guidelines in our frontend work.

6
Understanding Angular Views and Models

In this chapter, we will see Angular in practice, covering all the concepts of the previous chapters and using good practice to create a scalable application. We will focus on modularization and refactor our example application this time using a robust Yeoman generator for MEAN applications.

At this point, you should already be comfortable with the creation of an API using Node, Express, and MongoDB and also with tools like Bower, Grunt, and Yeoman, then we create our sample application. The following topics are covered in this chapter:

- Dissecting and understanding the MEAN.JS generator
- Scaffolding the application
- The application anatomy
- Refactoring the API
- Testing the speakers' API routes

Dissecting and understanding the MEAN.JS generator

On a MEAN stack environment, our ecosystem is infinitely diverse, and we can find excellent alternatives to start working with RESTful APIs. We have at our hand simple boilerplates to complex code generators that can be used with other tools in an integrated way, or even alone.

Boilerplates are usually a group of tested code and are modified to provide the basic structure to the main goal and create a foundation for a web application project. Besides saving us from common tasks such as assembling the basic structure of the code and organizing the files, boilerplates already has a number of scripts and snippets ready to go.

Let's describe an alternative that we consider as a good starting point for the development of RESTful APIs with the Express framework, MongoDB database, Node server, and AngularJS.

Differentiating MEAN.JS and MEAN.io

MEAN.JS is the most popular boilerplate that is currently available. It is a fork of the original project MEAN.io, both open source with a very peculiar curiosity and have the same author. For more details, check out `http://meanjs.org/`.

However, there are some differences. MEAN.JS consists of better code organization and structure of directories. Furthermore, it follows a vertical modularization system, thus facilitating the organization of code in decoupled modules with a more complete and robust environment.

The most common problem when we need to scale a SPA is undoubtedly the structure of directories that we adopt and how we manage all JavaScript files, when using the MVC/MVVM approach.

MEAN.JS provides the Angular framework with more flexibility to deal with the MVC approach for the frontend application, as we'll see inside the `public` folder. In the modules approach, each module has their own structure, maintaining some conventions for controllers, services, views, config, and tests.

 The `public` folder contains all the frontend files of application.

This flexibility is very useful for team development and keeps the project structure well organized. Besides, we have the power of subgenerators for almost all kinds of tasks such as creating routes, controllers, services, and directives.

Scaffolding the application

As already mentioned before, we use as tools as possible that streamline our development process of web applications.

We will start from scratch, using a Yeoman generator called MEAN.JS.

Let's begin; remember that you can download the sample files and follow our evolution. However, I strongly recommend that you follow refactoring step by step for a better understanding.

1. Create a folder called `meanjs-generator`, open the terminal inside it, and type:

   ```
   npm install -g generator-meanjs
   ```

   The `-g` key means general, and you'll need to be the administrator of your machine. Now, we have what we need: the generator.

2. Type the `yo meanjs` command and follow the instructions and fill in the answers; the text in light blue is the answer that you must complete, as shown in the following screenshot:

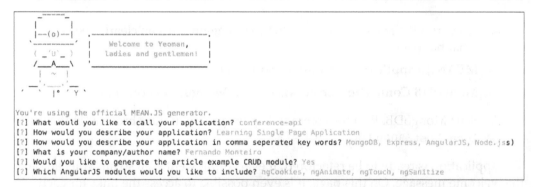

   If you accompany the process on your terminal, you can see that the Bower also already executed these commands and installed all the AngularJS scripts.

   All Yeoman generators have their own configuration options, and they are very easy to follow.

3. The next step is to run the `node server` command. Probably, you should receive an error message on your terminal, with some URLs pointing to MongoDB folders. In fact, it is predictable because it indicates that MongoDB is not running.

4. Then, open the `server.js` file on the application root and add a treatment for this error.

5. Include the following lines directly after the `var db = mongoose.connect(config.db);` line:

```
// Add a warning message if MongoDB don't running
mongoose.connection.on('error', function() {
    console.error('MongoDB Connection Error. Make sure MongoDB is
running.');
});
```

As shown in the following screenshot:

```
13
14    // Bootstrap db connection
15    var db = mongoose.connect(config.db);
16    // Add a warning message if MongoDB dont running
17    mongoose.connection.on('error', function() {
18        console.error('MongoDB Connection Error. Make sure MongoDB is running.');
19    });
20
```

6. Now, run the `node server.js` command again. We can clearly see what happened:

    MEAN.JS application started on port 3000

    MongoDB Connection Error. Make sure MongoDB is running.

7. Start MongoDB. Run the command again and open your browser in the `localhost:3000` URL.

The application is ready to be refactored; if everything went well so far, you can see the welcome message. On this page, it is even possible to access the links for each technology used and also the MEAN.JS documentation.

The application anatomy

This generator has a very important peculiarity. Usually, when we work with web applications using AngularJS, by default all application files reside in the `app` directory. However, in this case, this directory stores files regarding our API, for example, server files, which are usually stored in the `server` folder.

We can clearly see the separation and organization of our code in folders such as `controllers`, `models`, `routes`, `tests`, and `views`. There is nothing new up to now because we have already used this same structure in previous chapters; the only difference is the addition of the `tests` directory, as shown in the following screenshot:

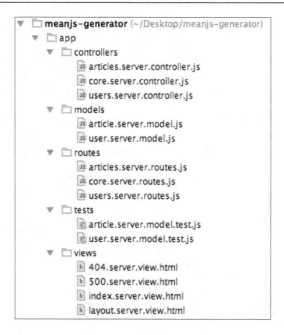

Note that the suffix, `server`, is present in the naming of all the files; it greatly facilitates the work of the team and became highly scalable. The `public` folder contains all files related to the frontend application. Note that each module has its own folder, in addition to all AngularJS files that are housed in the `lib` folder. Each module has its own internal structure to their respective folders: `config`, `controllers`, `services`, `tests`, `views`, and a file in the root that registers the module in the application, as shown in the following screenshot:

We cannot say that this is a simple structure. On the contrary, it is a complex but very well-divided structure. Finally, we have the `config` folder and two other folders inside it, `env` and `strategy`; the latter contains the configuration files of the Passport module to deal with authentication and user's control over Facebook, Google, LinkedIn, Twitter, and local access with a username and password.

The `env` directory holds settings, access to static files, template rendering, and session control in the `all.js` file. The other files store the connection string to the database and also the access keys for social networking APIs.

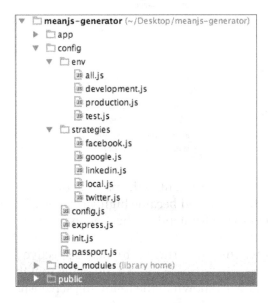

We shall now see briefly what each file's root folder is:

- `.bowerrec`: As we saw before setup, this is a file to receive Bower components

- `.gitignore`: This file doesn't track files on the control version

- `bower.json`: This file sets up the dependencies for the frontend side, such as Angular, jQuery, and Bootstrap

- `gruntfile.js`: This file is a task runner for building, testing, development, and other common tasks

- `karma.conf.js`: This file sets up the testing environment

- `license.md`: This file shows which license is used

- `package.json`: This sets up the application dependencies for server side, such as Express and Passport

- `procfile`: This sets up an environment for cloud deployment
- `readme.md`: This has information about the application
- `server.js`: As we saw before, this is the heart of the Node server for the application

We note that in this way, we can scale the application in a practical way. As we saw in the previous examples, we are ready to proceed with the refactoring. We will divide it into two stages: the first to the API, including a service for inclusion of speakers, and the second to create the frontend itself with AngularJS.

However, we can choose to create everything from scratch, including file-by-file directories in the backend and the frontend too. However, once you have already used the generator to create all this structure, use a subgenerator for creation of two steps (backend files and frontend files) simultaneously. This way, we save time and become more productive.

Refactoring the API

Let's see how we can create both tasks at the same time with the help of the subgenerator CRUD module:

1. In the terminal, type the following command:

   `yo meanjs:crud-module speakers`

   Note that the last word is the name we give to the module that will be created.

 More information about the MEAN.JS generator and sub-generator CRUD can be found at `http://meanjs.org/generator.html#crud-module`.

   After the process, we have the following information on the terminal window:

```
[?] Which supplemental folders would you like to include in your angular module? directives, filters
[?] Would you like to add the CRUD module links to a menu? Yes
[?] What is your menu identifier? Speakers
  create app/controllers/speakers.server.controller.js
  create app/models/speaker.server.model.js
  create app/routes/speakers.server.routes.js
  create app/tests/speaker.server.model.test.js
  create public/modules/speakers/config/speakers.client.routes.js
  create public/modules/speakers/controllers/speakers.client.controller.js
  create public/modules/speakers/services/speakers.client.service.js
  create public/modules/speakers/tests/speakers.client.controller.test.js
  create public/modules/speakers/config/speakers.client.config.js
  create public/modules/speakers/views/create-speaker.client.view.html
  create public/modules/speakers/views/edit-speaker.client.view.html
  create public/modules/speakers/views/list-speakers.client.view.html
  create public/modules/speakers/views/view-speaker.client.view.html
  create public/modules/speakers/speakers.client.module.js
```

Note that we respond to the three optional questions while creating the new module: whether we want to include a folder for CSS and images and two directories for Angular, directives and filters. For the purpose of this example, we chose not to include the directories of CSS and images; we will see why later.

 Don't forget to keep the server running with the node server command each time you need to test something on the browser; if you don't do so, use nodemon.

2. Now, let's test what we created. Open the browser and type localhost:3000. If you are using the Version 0.1.5 of the MEAN.JS generator, you will probably receive the following error:

Error: Menu does not exists

http://localhost:3000/modules/core/services/menus.client.service. js:35&host=localhost:3000

Surely this little bug will be fixed in the next release; however, now we will solve this manually.

3. Open the speaker.client.config.js file.

```
// Configuring the Articles module and replace the
    following code:
angular.module('speakers').run(['Menus',
function(Menus) {
    // Set top bar menu items
    Menus.addMenuItem('Speakers', 'Speakers', 'speakers',
    'dropdown', '/speakers(/create)?');
    Menus.addSubMenuItem('Speakers', 'speakers', 'List
    Speakers', 'speakers');
    Menus.addSubMenuItem('Speakers', 'speakers', 'New
    Speaker', 'speakers/create');
}
]);
```

4. Replace the preceding code with the following code:

```
// Configuring the Speakers module
angular.module('speakers').run(['Menus',
function(Menus) {
    // Set top bar menu items
    Menus.addMenuItem('topbar', 'Speakers', 'speakers',
    'dropdown', '/speakers(/create)?');
    Menus.addSubMenuItem('topbar', 'speakers', 'List
    Speakers', 'speakers');
```

```
Menus.addSubMenuItem('topbar', 'speakers', 'New Speaker',
'speakers/create');
}
]);
```

We changed the first parameter from the `Menus` function from `Speakers` to `topbar`, pretty simple.

5. Go back to the terminal and type the `node server` command again. Open the browser and type `localhost:3000`, and then log in or register a new user.

Finally, we can see our speakers menu item created, along with two submenus to list and add the speakers. This subgenerator is very similar to the Ruby on Rails scaffold, and even though we use it to create the necessary CRUD operations, we still have much work ahead.

We will make some simple alterations in the layout; the important parts will be highlighted:

1. Edit the home view template file located at `public/core/views/home.client.view.html`.

2. Open the file and delete all the content. After this, place the following code. Pay attention to the comments in the code; they indicate important areas of our application:

```html
<section data-ng-controller="HomeController" data-ng-init="find()">
<div class="jumbotron text-center">
  <div class="row">
    <div class="col-md-6 col-md-offset-3 col-sm-6 col-sm-offset-3 col-xs-12">
    <h1>Conference</h1>
    </div>
  </div>
  <br>
  <div class="row">
    <p class="lead">
    SPA applications with MEAN open conference.
    </p>
  </div>
  <div class="row">
    <p>
    <a class="btn btn-primary btn-lg" href="#!/signup">
    Call for Papers</a>
    </p>
```

```
        </div>
      </div>
      <section>
        <div class="page-header">
          <h1>Speakers</h1>
        </div>
        <div class="list-group">
          <!-- Add filter to list speakers by created date -->
          <a data-ng-repeat="speaker in speakers | filter:query
          | orderBy: 'created'" data-ng-
          href="#!/speakers/{{speaker._id}}" class="list-group-
          item">
            <img gravatar-src-once="speaker.email" class="list-
            group-item" style="float:left; margin-right: 10px;">
            <h4 class="list-group-item-heading"> <span data-ng-
            bind="speaker.name"></span></h4>
            <h5 class="list-group-item-heading text-primary">
            Track : <span data-ng-
            bind="speaker.title"></span></h5>
            <p> Description: <span data-ng-
            bind="speaker.description"></span></p>
            <p class="list-group-item"> Time: <span data-ng-
            bind="speaker.schedule"></span></p>
          </a>
        </div>
        <!-- Add a simple message if don't have any speaker yet
        -->
        <div class="alert alert-warning text-center" data-ng-
        hide="!speakers.$resolved || speakers.length">
          No Speakers yet, why don't you
          <a href="/#!/speakers/create">create one</a>?
        </div>
      </section>
    </section>
    <footer>
      <p class="text-center">Conference &copy; 2014</p>
    </footer>
```

Let's check what happened in the preceding code:

- The first line with `data-ng-init="find()"` can be `ng-init="find()"`; the `data` attribute is very useful for some HTML5 validators

- The `find()` function inside `ng-init` is just a function to list all the speakers

- The `ng-repeat` directive has another AngularJS keyword, the `filter` feature, which we saw in *Chapter 5, Starting with AngularJS*

- ○ The `img gravatar-src-once="speaker.email"` directive is the `angular-gravatar` directive, which we will see in the next section

- ○ The `data-ng-hide="!speakers.$resolved || speakers.length"` directive activates an error message if there isn't any registered speaker

3. Edit the authentication redirection. So, open the `authentication.client.controller.js` file located at `public/modules/users/controllers/authentication.client.controller.js` and go to the `$scope.sign` function and add the following line right after `$scope.authentication.user = response;`:

```
//And redirect to the index page
$location.path('/speakers');
```

4. With this alteration, after the login page, we are directed to the speakers' page instead of the index page. The complete function looks like this:

```
$scope.signin = function() {
  $http.post('/auth/signin',
  $scope.credentials).success(function(response) {
    //If successful we assign the response to the global
    user model
    $scope.authentication.user = response;

    //And redirect to the index page
    $location.path('/speakers');
  }).error(function(response) {
    $scope.error = response.message;
    });
};
```

5. Edit the home controller. So, open the `home.client.controller.js` file at `public/modules/core/controllers/home.client.controller.js`

6. Add the following lines, just after `$scope.authentication = Authentication;`:

```
// Find a list of Speakers
$scope.find = function() {
  $scope.speakers = Speakers.query();
};
```

7. Add the `speakers` module to the controller parameters:

```
angular.module('core').controller('HomeController',
['$scope', 'Authentication', 'Speakers',
function($scope, Authentication, Speakers) {}
```

The whole module looks like this:

```
angular.module('core').controller('HomeController',
['$scope', 'Authentication', 'Speakers',
function($scope, Authentication, Speakers) {
  // This provides Authentication context.
  $scope.authentication = Authentication;

  // Find a list of Speakers
  $scope.find = function() {
    $scope.speakers = Speakers.query();
    };
}
]);
```

With this, we can list all the speakers in the index page.

The last action necessary to conclude this step is the installation of a module called `angular-gravatar`. We open a parenthesis here to describe in a few lines what this module is.

The result we hope to get is shown in the following screenshot:

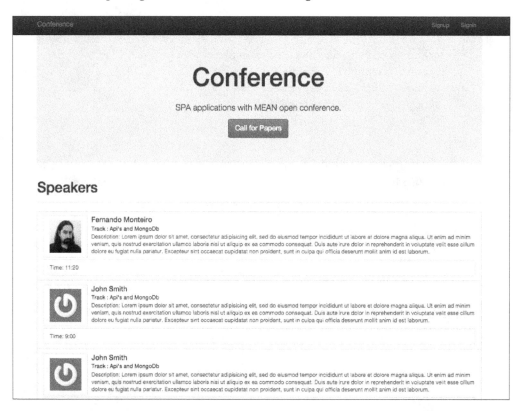

Don't worry about the data; we will see how to place the data later in next topics.

The angular-gravatar image directive

Imagine an application receiving hundreds of inscriptions to call for papers, and consequently we can use the application for long-duration events, making it a monthly event with 10 speakers per day for 30 days with an average of 300 entries, each with a photo of your speaker.

Our server must be prepared to receive and handle this amount of images. For this, we use the known service called Gravatar (`http://en.gravatar.com/`), where you can register an image (Avatar) and an e-mail account and use their API for integration with blogs and other systems.

 More information about `angular-gravatar` can be found at `https://github.com/wallin/angular-gravatar`.

Here, we will use `angular-gravatar`; so this way, the speaker must enter your e-mail address and the module takes care of the rest.

Let's see how this works in practice:

1. Open your terminal and type:

   ```
   bower install angular-gravatar --save
   ```

2. Add `md5.js` and `angular-gravatar.js` to the application in `config/env/all.js` the file, right at the end of AngularJS dependencies:

   ```
   'public/lib/angular-gravatar/build/md5.min.js',
   'public/lib/angular-gravatar/build/angular-gravatar.min.js'
   ```

    Note that all the script tags go here in this file.

3. In `public/config.js`, add the following code to the `var applicationModuleVendorDependencies` array:

   ```
   ui.gravatar
   ```

4. Edit the `list-speakers.client.view.html` file located at `public/modules/speakers/views/list-speakers.client.view.html`

5. Replace the code with the following code:

```
<section data-ng-controller="SpeakersController" data-ng-
init="find()">
  <div class="page-header">
    <h1>Speakers</h1>
  </div>
  <div class="list-group">
    <a data-ng-repeat="speaker in speakers" data-ng-
    href="#!/speakers/{{speaker._id}}/edit" class="list-
    group-item">
    <img gravatar-src-once="speaker.email" class="list-
    group-item" style="float:left; margin-right: 10px;">
    <h4 class="list-group-item-heading">
    <span data-ng-bind="speaker.name"></span></h4>
    <h5 class="list-group-item-heading">
    Track : <span data-ng-bind="speaker.title"></span></h5>
    <p> Description: <span
    data-ng-bind="speaker.description"></span></p>
    <p class="list-group-item">
    Time: <span data-ng-bind="speaker.schedule"></span></p>
    </a>
  </div>
  <div class="alert alert-warning text-center"
    data-ng-hide="!speakers.$resolved || speakers.length">
    No Speakers yet, why don't you
    <a href="/#!/speakers/create">create one</a>?
  </div>
</section>
```

Note the img tag with gravatar-src-once="speaker.email" with the source binding to the e-mail field. This is where the magic happens.

6. Edit the edit-speakers.client.view.html file located at public/modules/speakers/views/edit-speakers.client.view.html and replace the code with the following code:

```
<section data-ng-controller="SpeakersController" data-ng-
init="findOne()">
  <div class="page-header">
    <h1>Edit Speaker</h1>
  </div>
  <div class="col-md-12">
    <div class="thumbnail">
      <img gravatar-src-once="speaker.email" alt="{{speaker.
name}}">
    </div>
```

```
<form class="form-horizontal" data-ng-submit="update()"
novalidate>
  <fieldset>
    <div class="form-group">
      <label class="control-label"
      for="name">Name</label>
      <div class="controls">
        <input type="text" data-ng-model="speaker.name"
        id="name" class="form-control"
        placeholder="Name" required>
      </div>
    </div>
    <div class="form-group">
      <label class="control-label"
        for="name">Title</label>
      <div class="controls">
        <input type="text"
        data-ng-model="speaker.title"
        id="title" class="form-control"
        placeholder="Titulo" required>
      </div>
    </div>
    <div class="form-group">
      <label class="control-label"
      for="description">Description</label>
      <div class="controls">
        <textarea data-ng-model="speaker.description"
        id="description" class="form-control"
        placeholder="Description" required></textarea>
      </div>
    </div>
    <div class="form-group">
      <label class="control-label"
      for="email">Email</label>
      <div class="controls">
        <input type="text"
        data-ng-model="speaker.email"
        id="email" class="form-control"
        placeholder="Email" required>
      </div>
    </div>
    <div class="form-group">
      <label class="control-label"
      for="schedule">Schedule</label>
      <div class="controls">
```

```
            <input type="text" data-ng-
            model="speaker.schedule" id="schedule"
            class="form-control" placeholder="Schedule"
            required>
          </div>
        </div>
        <div class="form-group">
          <input type="submit" value="Update" class="btn
          btn-success">
          <a class="btn btn-danger"
          data-ng-click="remove();">Delete</a>
        </div>
        <div data-ng-show="error" class="text-danger">
          <strong data-ng-bind="error"></strong>
        </div>
      </fieldset>
    </form>
  </div>
</section>
```

Here, we use the Angular expression, `<img gravatar-src-once="speaker.` `email" alt="{{speaker.name}}">`, to insert the speaker's name inside the `alt` image attribute.

7. Edit the `create-speakers.client.view.html` file located at `public/` `modules/speakers/views/create-speakers.client.view.html` and replace the code with the following code:

```
<section data-ng-controller="SpeakersController">
  <div class="page-header">
    <h1>New Speaker</h1>
  </div>
  <div class="col-md-12">
    <img gravatar-src-once="email" alt="{{name}}">
    <form class="form-horizontal" data-ng-submit="create()"
    novalidate>
      <fieldset>
        <div class="form-group">
          <label class="control-label"
          for="name">Name</label>
          <div class="controls">
            <input type="text" data-ng-model="name"
            id="name" class="form-control"
            placeholder="Name" required>
          </div>
        </div>
```

```
        <div class="form-group">
          <label class="control-label"
          for="title">Title</label>
          <div class="controls">
            <input type="text" data-ng-model="title"
            id="title" class="form-control"
            placeholder="Title" required>
          </div>
        </div>
        <div class="form-group">
          <label class="control-label"
          for="description">Description</label>
          <div class="controls">
            <textarea data-ng-model="description"
            id="description" class="form-control"
            placeholder="description" required></textarea>
          </div>
        </div>
        <div class="form-group">
          <label class="control-label"
          for="email">Email</label>
          <div class="controls">
            <input type="text" data-ng-model="email"
            id="email" class="form-control"
            placeholder="email" required>
          </div>
        </div>
        <div class="form-group">
          <label class="control-label"
          for="schedule">Schedule</label>
          <div class="controls">
            <input type="text" data-ng-model="schedule"
            id="schedule" class="form-control"
            placeholder="schedule" required>
          </div>
        </div>
        <div class="form-group">
          <input type="submit" class="btn btn-default">
        </div>
        <div data-ng-show="error" class="text-danger">
          <strong data-ng-bind="error"></strong>
        </div>
      </fieldset>
    </form>
  </div>
</section>
```

The create form is different from the list form in `<img gravatar-src-once="email" alt="{{name}}">`, because here we don't have the speaker yet; so the `{{name}}` expression is from `data-ng-model="name"`.

8. Edit the `view-speakers.client.view.html` file located at `public/modules/speakers/views/view-speakers.client.view.html` and replace the code with the following code:

```
<section data-ng-controller="SpeakersController" data-ng-
init="findOne()">
  <div class="page-header">
    <div class="row">
      <div class="col-md-12">
        <div class="thumbnail">
          <img gravatar-src-once="speaker.email"
          alt="{{speaker.name}}">
          <div class="caption">
            <h3 class="text-center"
            data-ng-bind="speaker.name"></h3>
            <h4 class="text-center"
            data-ng-bind="speaker.title"></h4>
            <p class="text-center"
            data-ng-bind="speaker.schedule"></p>
            <p class="text-justify"
            data-ng-bind="speaker.description"></p>
          </div>
          <small>
            <em class="text-muted">Posted on
            <span data-ng-bind="speaker.created |
            date:'mediumDate'"></span> by
            <span data-ng-
            bind="speaker.user.displayName"></span>
            </em>
          </small>
        </div>
        <div class="btn-group btn-group-justified"
        data-ng-show="authentication.user._id ==
        speaker.user._id">
          <div class="btn-group">
            <a class="btn btn-default"
            href="/#!/speakers/{{speaker._id}}/edit">
            <i class="glyphicon glyphicon-edit"></i> Edit
            </a>
          </div>
          <div class="btn-group">
```

```
        <a class="btn btn-default"
        data-ng-click="remove();">
        <i class="glyphicon glyphicon-trash"></i>
        Delete
        </a>
      </div>
    </div>
  </div>
  </div>
</section>
```

The highlighted code checks whether the user is logged in; if so, show the **Edit** and **Delete** buttons, and if not, just show the speaker page.

9. Edit the speaker model file app/models/speaker/speaker.server.model. html and replace the code with the following code:

```
'use strict';

/**
 * Module dependencies.
 */
var mongoose = require('mongoose'),
Schema = mongoose.Schema;

/**
 * Speaker Schema
 */
var SpeakerSchema = new Schema({
  name: {
    type: String,
    default: '',
    trim: true,
    required: 'Name cannot be blank'
  },
  title: {
    type: String,
    default: ''
  },
  description: {
    type: String,
    default: ''
  },
  schedule: {
```

```
      type: String,
      default:''
    },
    email: {
      type: String,
      default:''
    },
    created: {
      type: Date,
      default: Date.now
    },
    user: {
      type: Schema.ObjectId,
      ref: 'User'
    }
});
```

```
mongoose.model('Speaker', SpeakerSchema);
```

The last highlighted field stores the actual user on speaker creation, as we can see in MongoDB:

```
{
    __v: 0,
    _id: ObjectId("54036bfff14a90fd02213d37"),
    created: ISODate("2014-08-31T18:39:59.444Z"),
    description: "Lorem ipsum dolor sit amet, consectetur
    adipiscing elit...",
    email: "",
    name: "John Master",
    schedule: "10:00",
    title: "MongoDB in depth",
    user: ObjectId("54034f440c486ebb02859637")
}
```

Our refactoring here was massive, but we do this because even though we use the CRUD generator, we still have much work to do, as mentioned earlier.

10. Lastly, insert the necessary fields to the speaker model that will be stored in the database with the Mongoose schema.

Now, let's insert some data in our API using Postman again.

 Note that you need to run the application and be logged in, to be able to enter data using Postman. Later, we will see how to pass the necessary credentials to enter data without being logged in to the application.

Follow the steps to insert data in our API:

1. You can enter any data in the fields on the right, but the fields on the left-hand side must keep the same names as the fields in the speakers' schema:

Now, we can access our application to see the result.

2. Open your browser and type `http://localhost:3000/`.

   After the login, you can see the speakers page and the thumbnail image from the `speakers` module imported from the Gravatar website. When you fill the e-mail field with a valid e-mail address, we have a speaker picture. When it is left blank, they assume the default Gravatar icon, as shown in the following screenshot:

Testing the speakers' API routes

As we saw in the previous chapters, to include data on the API, we use Postman. Now, we will see another way to accomplish RESTful tests and how to insert data without being logged in.

This time, we will use the WebStorm IDE to test the RESTful API.

To trigger the RESTful tests panel, click on **Tools** and then on **Test RESTful Web Service**; this will activate the test panel.

With the panel enabled, let's insert some data, an HTTP method, a host, and a path, which in our case is `/speakers`.

First, we test the POST method. For this, we must fill some information in the **Request Parameters** pane, as shown in the following screenshot:

Note that the necessary credentials for this operation are on the **Cookies** tab, as shown in the following screenshot.

If you try to perform this same operation using Postman without being logged into the application, you will receive a message that says **this User is not logged in**.

This is very useful as you do not need to be logged in to perform application testing and populate the database. We just need a valid session cookie.

Summary

One more trip to the universe of SPA; in this chapter, we saw the best use of a code generator.

We went through the anatomy of large-scale applications using JavaScript on the server side and on the frontend.

We refactored part of the whole frontend with AngularJS, applying key concepts we saw in the previous chapter such as directives and filters.

We also learned how to use the Webstorm IDE to test applications based on the RESTful web services.

In the next chapter, we will see the importance and the architecture of the tests that employ AngularJS and how to use and configure Karma and Protractor, among other things.

7
Testing Angular SPA with Karma and Protractor

In this chapter, we'll dive a bit deeper into the AngularJS Framework and understand some very important points about testing on SPA.

As we mentioned in the previous chapters, SPA transfers MVC responsibility to JavaScript that runs on the client side (the browser). We must write the tests in the same way as we do when dealing with MVC on server-side languages.

The AngularJS framework is designed to be highly testable and because of that we have some tools that facilitate this process. Today, writing test cases is part of the web development process of every programmer, whether frontend or backend. Test-driven development is part of all agile methodologies and you should remember this. The sooner you start writing tests, the better it will be for you.

In the upcoming sections, we will see some basic concepts of tests, such as unit testing and integration testing (known as e2e testing) among other things. These are as follows:

- Testing concepts
- Introducing Jasmine
- Configuring Karma (unit testing)
- Running a Karma test
- Configuring Protractor (e2e testing)
- Running Protractor testing

Testing concepts

Let's focus on the two types of tests that will be covered in our sample application: unit testing and e2e testing. A very interesting fact to note here is that previously most of the frontend developers did not worry about tests. Testing was exclusively done by the testing team or quality assurance department. However, the reality has changed now. It is hard to find test teams with even a basic knowledge of JavaScript to perform the necessary tests on SPAs. When I mention test, it means automated testing. The reason why we consider an automated test is that when your application grows from medium to large scale, it will become very complicated to test all interfaces with new implementations.

Currently, frontend developers are more concerned with how to write JavaScript, and how to apply concepts of **Test-Driven Development (TDD)** and **Behavior-Driven Development (BDD)**.

The following diagram illustrates the workflow of TDD:

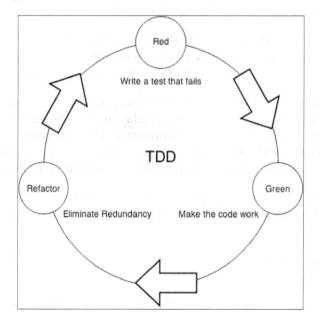

The concept of TDD is directly related to the techniques of extreme programming, where the developer creates small test cases for a given functionality, then implements the code for it to respond, and pass the test. This kind of pattern is directly related to the unit tests; of course, there are many other things about unit testing and TDD, but these terms are fine to understand the importance. Also, unit tests help the developer to maintain focus on what is really important.

On the other side, we have BDD (widely used in agile software development), which allows you to integrate the entire team with developers and business people. This does not use technical language to describe certain expected behaviors of the system interface.

The main idea is to write small blocks of tests, and then write the necessary code to pass the tests. This procedure is of utmost importance in an agile development because the code must be readable to be maintained and easy to scale.

Unit tests are very useful to test small blocks of code, but when we need to perform tests on a set of all of these small blocks, then we need to think of the behavior we expect from the interface. For this, we use e2e testing. So, the main purpose of writing code with tests in mind is to produce code that is easily maintainable, understandable for humans, debuggable, and bug free.

Although this is not an everyday practice for frontend developers, TDD is very useful when it comes to software development in general. It is extremely suitable when using any MVC or MVVM pattern.

So, let's see how we can implement tests on our SPA.

The AngularJS framework was built and planned with testing in mind, so we have a lot of options to choose from with regards to frameworks. The forthcoming examples will talk about the Karma and Protractor test runner.

Introducing Jasmine

Karma is one of the most commonly used tools for test execution; it is compatible with many testing frameworks (such as Mocha, QUnit, and Jasmine). You can use it to test any JavaScript code, and it is highly recommended that you use some tool to test and perform automated testing on SPA.

In the following examples, we will be using Jasmine to write the tests and Karma to run the test. Jasmine has a very simple and easy writing syntax. Also, it is not dependent on any other framework. A basic example of writing tests looks like the following code:

```
describe("The test name", function() {
  it("contains spec with an expectation", function() {
    expect(true).toBe(true);
  });
});
```

describe() and it() are two functions. The describe() function has two parameters: a string parameter that receives the name of the test, and a function parameter that implements the spec using the it() function. The expect() function is a matcher function to get a result. The matcher function receives a boolean value comparison between the actual value and the expected value. Here is a simple example to understand matcher with an expect() function:

```
describe("How matchers works:", function() {

    it("The 'toBe' matcher compares with ===", function() {
        var number = 12;
        var letter = a;

        expect(number).toBe(letter);
        expect(number).not.toBe(null);
    });
});
```

Matcher is very useful; we can create our own matcher if necessary.

We can use the describe() function to group related specs to test an entire module like the following example:

```
describe("Login test series", function() {
    it("Try to login with blank user", function() {
        ...
    });

    it("Try to login with wrong user", function() {
        ...
    });
    // More it() functions goes here.
});
```

The Jasmine API is pretty easy to understand; it has several other functions, but this baseline is enough to understand the following examples.

 To find out more about the Jasmine test framework, refer to http://jasmine.github.io/.

Let's take a look at the Karma test runner and how to start using it.

 We will not cover the necessary steps to install Karma and its modules; you can download the entire project from the examples and install all the necessary dependencies with the following command on the application root folder:

npm install

Configuring Karma (unit testing)

Karma is configured with a file called `karma.conf.js`.

 You can find more information about Karma at `http://karma-runner.github.io/0.12/index.html`.

The easiest way to create this file is to use the karma-cli tool. This way, you will have the `init` command available in your terminal. This is a standard procedure used in many tools available for Node.js environments, such as Grunt, Bower, and some others.

Command line interface (**CLI**) helps us to create files and settings in a simple and fast way using the terminal. As we already have the `karma.conf.js` file, we don't need to perform the `init` command.

Open the project folder. Now, let's review the `karma.conf.js` file to understand it line by line:

```
'use strict';

/**
 * Module dependencies.
 */
var applicationConfiguration = require('./config/config');

// Karma configuration
module.exports = function(config) {
  config.set({
    // Frameworks to use
    frameworks: ['jasmine'],
```

```
        // List of files / patterns to load in the browser
        files: applicationConfiguration.assets.lib.js.concat(applicationCo
    nfiguration.assets.js, applicationConfiguration.assets.tests),

        // Test results reporter to use
        // Possible values: 'dots', 'progress', 'junit', 'growl',
        'coverage'
        //reporters: ['progress'],
        reporters: ['progress'],

        // Web server port
        port: 9876,

        // Enable / disable colors in the output (reporters and logs)
        colors: true,

        // Level of logging
        // Possible values: config.LOG_DISABLE || config.LOG_ERROR ||
        config.LOG_WARN || config.LOG_INFO || config.LOG_DEBUG
        logLevel: config.LOG_INFO,

        // Enable / disable watching file and executing tests whenever
        any file changes
        autoWatch: true,

        // Start these browsers, currently available:
        // - Chrome
        // - ChromeCanary
        // - Firefox
        // - Opera
        // - Safari (only Mac)
        // - PhantomJS
        // - IE (only Windows)
        browsers: ['PhantomJS'],

        // If browser does not capture in given timeout [ms], kill it
        captureTimeout: 60000,

        // Continuous Integration mode
        // If true, it capture browsers, run tests and exit
        singleRun: true
    });
};
```

The highlighted code tells Karma about the location of the test files and whether it is the same as the following code:

```
// list of files / patterns to load in the browser
files: [
  'public/**/*.test.js'
],
```

The `applicationConfiguration` variable was set up before the Karma function with the following code:

```
var applicationConfiguration = require('./config/config');
```

Note that we are using the Jasmine framework as we mentioned before. At this point, we already have the necessary baseline to start writing tests.

Reviewing the speaker controller test

We might notice that all modules already have their respective folders called `tests`. This is because when we use the Yeoman generator, it already creates these configurations. All the necessary files for the controllers, services, directives, and tests are already stored, as seen previously. So we already have our boilerplate ready to test.

Then, we will review it so that we can fix the procedure we have performed. Open the file `speakers.client.controller.test.js` in `public/modules/speakers/tests/`.

We will discuss some blocks of code for a better understanding of what is happening step-by-step. Then, we will insert some additional comments that are not present in the original file to understand what is happening with each part of the code. Further, we will be using the same concepts that we saw earlier in the introductory section of Jasmine. The `describe()` function receives the test name and a function parameter with the test itself, as shown in the following code:

```
(function() {
  // Speakers Controller Spec
  describe('Speakers Controller Tests', function() {
    // Initialize global variables
    var SpeakersController,
    scope,
    $httpBackend,
    $stateParams,
    $location;
  });
});
```

In this function, we initialize some global variables. Note that we use the $ sign to set AngularJS features (such as $httpBackend, $stateParams, and $location). The $resource service augments the response object with methods to update and delete the resource. If we were to use the standard toEqual matcher, our tests would fail because the test values will not exactly match the responses. To solve this problem, we define a new toEqualData Jasmine matcher. When the toEqualData matcher compares two objects, it takes only object properties into account and ignores methods, as shown in the following code:

```
beforeEach(function() {
    jasmine.addMatchers({
        toEqualData: function(util, customEqualityTesters) {
            return {
                compare: function(actual, expected) {
                    return {
                        pass: angular.equals(actual, expected)
                    };
                }
            };
        }
    });
});

// Then we can start by loading the main application module
beforeEach(module
(ApplicationConfiguration.applicationModuleName));

// The injector ignores leading and trailing underscores here
(i.e. _$httpBackend_).
// This allows us to inject a service but then attach it to a
variable
// with the same name as the service.
beforeEach(inject(function($controller, $rootScope,
_$location_, _$stateParams_, _$httpBackend_) {
    // Set a new global scope
    scope = $rootScope.$new();

    // Point global variables to injected services
    $stateParams = _$stateParams_;
    $httpBackend = _$httpBackend_;
    $location = _$location_;

    // Initialize the Speakers controller.
    SpeakersController = $controller('SpeakersController', {
        $scope: scope
    });
}));
```

Here, note the use of the `beforeEach()` function. The name is very intuitive; we use this function to start some procedure before each test. The first use of the `beforeEach()` function on the code sample is to add the new matcher `toEqualData`, the second use is to load the application configuration, and the third use is to inject the AngularJS directives.

Now, we use the `it()` function to describe what we expect from the test; the highlighted string shows this:

```
it('$scope.find() should create an array with at least one Speaker
object fetched from XHR', inject(function(Speakers) {
    // Create sample Speaker using the Speakers service
    var sampleSpeaker = new Speakers({
      name: 'New Speaker',
      title: '',
      description: '',
      email: '',
      schedule: ''
    });
```

Note that we add the highlighted properties to the `sampleSpeaker` object. Do the same in your file by performing the following steps:

1. Add the properties, namely, `title`, `description`, `email`, and `schedule` to the `sampleSpeaker` object using the following code:

```
// Create a sample Speakers array that includes the new
Speaker
var sampleSpeakers = [sampleSpeaker];

// Set GET response
$httpBackend.expectGET('speakers').respond
(sampleSpeakers);

// Run controller functionality
scope.find();
$httpBackend.flush();

// Test scope value
expect(scope.speakers).toEqualData(sampleSpeakers);
}));
```

2. The second `it()` function is used to find a specific speaker using `speakerId`:

```
it('$scope.findOne() should create an array with one
    Speaker The object fetched from XHR using a speakerId URL
    parameter', inject(function(Speakers) {
```

```
    // Define a sample Speaker object
    var sampleSpeaker = new Speakers({
      name: 'New Speaker',
      title: '',
      description: '',
      email: '',
      schedule: ''
    });
```

3. Add the properties, namely, `title`, `description`, `email`, and `schedule` to
   the previous `sampleSpeaker` object using the following code:

```
    // Set the URL parameter
    $stateParams.speakerId = '525a8422f6d0f87f0e407a33';

    // Set GET response
    $httpBackend.expectGET(/speakers\/([0-9a-fA-
    F]{24})$/).respond(sampleSpeaker);

    // Run controller functionality
    scope.findOne();
    $httpBackend.flush();

    // Test scope value
    expect(scope.speaker).toEqualData(sampleSpeaker);
    }));
```

4. The third `it()` function is used to create a speaker:

```
    it('$scope.create() with valid form data should send a POST
      request with the form input values and then locate to new
      object URL', inject(function(Speakers) {
      // Create a sample Speaker object
      var sampleSpeakerPostData = new Speakers({
        name: 'New Speaker',
        title: 'Title Test',
        description: 'Description Test',
        email: 'email@test.com',
        schedule: '11:00'
      });

      // Create a sample Speaker response
      var sampleSpeakerResponse = new Speakers({
        _id: '525cf20451979dea2c000001',
        name: 'New Speaker',
        title: 'Title Test',
```

```
    description: 'Description Test',
    email: 'email@test.com',
    schedule: '11:00'
});
```

5. Add the properties, namely, `title`, `description`, `email`, and `schedule` to the `sampleSpeakerPostData` object and `sampleSpeakerResponse` object like the previous highlighted code:

```
// Fixture mock form input values
scope.name = 'New Speaker';
scope.title = 'Title Test';
scope.description = 'Description Test';
scope.email = 'email@test.com';
scope.schedule = '11:00'
```

6. Add the properties, namely, `title`, `description`, `email`, and `schedule` to the fixture mock form like the previous highlighted code:

```
// Set POST response
$httpBackend.expectPOST('speakers',
sampleSpeakerPostData).respond(sampleSpeakerResponse);

// Run controller functionality
scope.create();
$httpBackend.flush();

// Test form inputs are reset
expect(scope.name).toEqual('');

// Test URL redirection after the Speaker was created
expect($location.path()).toBe('/speakers/' +
sampleSpeakerResponse._id);
    }));
```

Until now, we have configured three `it()` functions to test speakers to get speakers, get speakers by id, and create methods to perform the CRUD operations. We need one function to test update a speaker, and another function to remove a speaker. Let's continue with the following steps:

1. The next test is to update an user, using the following code:

```
it('$scope.update() should update a valid Speaker',
inject(function(Speakers) {
    // Define a sample Speaker put data
    var sampleSpeakerPutData = new Speakers({
      _id: '525cf20451979dea2c000001',
```

```
                name: 'New Speaker',
                    title: 'Update the Text',
                    description: 'Update the Description',
                    email: 'update@test.com',
                    schedule: '10:00'
        });
```

2. Add the properties, namely, `title`, `description`, `email`, and `schedule` to the `sampleSpeakerPutData` object like the previous highlighted code:

```
// Mock Speaker in scope
scope.speaker = sampleSpeakerPutData;

// Set PUT response
$httpBackend.expectPUT(/speakers\/([0-9a-fA-
F]{24})$/).respond();

// Run controller functionality
scope.update();
$httpBackend.flush();

// Test URL location to new object
expect($location.path()).toBe('/speakers/' +
sampleSpeakerPutData._id);
    }));
```

3. The last `it()` function is used to remove a speaker:

```
it('$scope.remove() should send a DELETE request with a
valid speakerId and remove the Speaker from the scope',
inject(function(Speakers) {
// Create new Speaker object
var sampleSpeaker = new Speakers({
  _id: '525a8422f6d0f87f0e407a33'
});

// Create new Speakers array and include the Speaker
scope.speakers = [sampleSpeaker];

// Set expected DELETE response
$httpBackend.expectDELETE(/speakers\/([0-9a-fA-
F]{24})$/).respond(204);
```

```
// Run controller functionality
scope.remove(sampleSpeaker);
$httpBackend.flush();

// Test array after successful delete
expect(scope.speakers.length).toBe(0);
    }));
```

At this point, we have already reviewed all the necessary functions to test the CRUD operations from the speaker controller. Also, we added the missing code to test all the properties that were added in the previous chapter, where we created the new speaker controller.

As we are using the MEAN.JS generator, we don't need to write the tests to the other controllers: articles, core, and users. Don't worry; the procedure applied to the speaker controller is the same as these files. Now, let's see how to run these tests with Karma.

Running a Karma test

Again, note that due to the use of the MEAN.JS generator, we do not need to configure the task to run Karma; we just need to trigger the Grunt.js task to do the job for us. Perform the following steps:

1. Open your terminal in the project root folder and type the following command:

    `grunt test`

2. As we are using the `grunt-karma` plugin, we just need the following code to write the Karma task on `Gruntfile`:

```
karma: {
    unit: {
      configFile: 'karma.conf.js'
    }
},
```

3. You should run the command line to start MongoDB. Although we are using the Compose.io platform to run the test, we need a local instance of the database since we are testing the sample application. Here is a screenshot from the terminal after all the tests pass:

```
Application loaded using the "test" environment configuration

MEAN.JS application started on port 3001


  Article Model Unit Tests:
    Method Save
      ✓ should be able to save without problems
      ✓ should be able to show an error when try to save without title

  Speaker Model Unit Tests:
    Method Save
      ✓ should be able to save without problems
      ✓ should be able to show an error when try to save without name

  User Model Unit Tests:
    Method Save
      ✓ should begin with no users
      ✓ should be able to save without problems (41ms)
      ✓ should fail to save an existing user again (79ms)
      ✓ should be able to show an error when try to save without first name


  8 passing (176ms)


Running "karma:unit" (karma) task
INFO [karma]: Karma v0.12.23 server started at http://localhost:9876/
INFO [launcher]: Starting browser PhantomJS
INFO [PhantomJS 1.9.7 (Mac OS X)]: Connected on socket VXybUtTjlRJ_T3pkzWqG with id 22658276
PhantomJS 1.9.7 (Mac OS X): Executed 17 of 17 SUCCESS (0.019 secs / 0.118 secs)
```

We can see that all the tests were successful, but we also note that eight tests that were successfully performed are on the API, and our tests are executed in the karma task: unit.

This is because the Grunt.js task performs all the tests configured in the `Gruntfile.js` file. So, let's see what we need to accomplish the unit tests on the speaker model.

Reviewing the speaker model test

Add the following lines of code to perform the model tests:

1. Open the file `speaker.server.model.test.js` in the `app/tests/` folder. Let's review the existing code and add some necessary lines of code to perform the tests:

```
'use strict';
```

```
/**
 * Module dependencies.
 */
var should = require('should'),
  mongoose = require('mongoose'),
  User = mongoose.model('User'),
  Speaker = mongoose.model('Speaker');

/**
 * Globals
 */
var user, speaker;

/**
 * Unit tests
 */
```

As we discussed before, the `describe()` function receives the test name as the first parameter, and the test itself is the second parameter. Here, we have a `beforeEach` function to create a user object and assign some default values in the following code:

```
describe('Speaker Model Unit Tests:', function() {
  beforeEach(function(done) {
    user = new User({
      firstName: 'Full',
      lastName: 'Name',
      displayName: 'Full Name',
      email: 'test@test.com',
      username: 'username',
      password: 'password'
    });

    user.save(function() {
      speaker = new Speaker({
        name: 'Speaker Name',
        title: 'Track Title',
        decription: 'description of the speaker track',
        email: 'testemail@test.com.br',
        schedule: '9:10',
        user: user
      });

      done();
    });
  });
```

2. Add the previous highlighted properties to the `save()` function, as shown in the following code:

```
describe('Method Save', function() {
    it('should be able to save without problems',
    function(done) {
      return speaker.save(function(err) {
        should.not.exist(err);
        done();
      });
    });

    it('should be able to show an error when try to save
    without name', function(done) {
      speaker.name = '';

      return speaker.save(function(err) {
        should.exist(err);
        done();
      });
    });
  });

  afterEach(function(done) {
    Speaker.remove().exec();
    User.remove().exec();

    done();
    });
  });
```

Note that we continue using the same Jasmine syntax as the previous tests to write the API tests. So, when we test the speakers' controller, we are inside the `public` folder, and when we test the speakers' model, we are inside the `app` folder, which covers tests in the frontend and backend code.

You can find the grunt-mocha test in the following code, which is extracted from the `gruntfile.js` file on the root application folder:

```
mochaTest: {
  src: watchFiles.mochaTests,
  options: {
    reporter: 'spec',
    require: 'server.js'
  }
},
```

The `watchFiles.mochaTests` property is the path to `app/tests/**/*.js`.

 More information about Mocha can be found at `http://mochajs.org/`.

For information about grunt-mocha, refer to `https://github.com/kmiyashiro/grunt-mocha`.

Karma testing with WebStorm

As we mentioned earlier, the WebStorm IDE provides support for several programming languages and frameworks, including tests that uses the Karma framework. To use this feature, simply right-click on the file **karma.conf.js**, and then select **Run 'karma.conf.js'** from the context menu, as shown in the following screenshot:

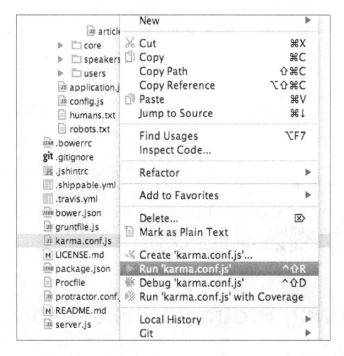

As we can see in the preceding screenshot, it is possible to run the tests using a **Coverage** option. Therefore, we need to make a small change in the Karma configuration file. Perform the following steps:

1. Open the `karma.conf.js` file from the root project folder.

2. Change the following highlighted code to use `coverage` instead of `progress`:

```
// Test results reporter to use
// Possible values: 'dots', 'progress', 'junit', 'growl',
'coverage'
//reporters: ['progress'],
reporters: ['coverage'],
```

3. Right-click on **karma.conf.js** and select **Run 'karma.conf.js' with Coverage**.

The result of the tests can be found in the following screenshot:

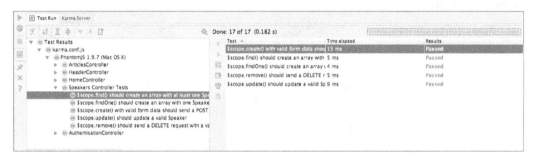

On the left panel, we can see the test cases for each controller, whereas on the right panel, we can see the test progress.

Talking about testing as a subject will require another book, since the scope of this book does not allow us to get into the details about the different frameworks for testing. However, what is described in this chapter is sufficient to begin the tests on SPA.

Configuring Protractor (e2e testing)

Protractor is a framework of functional tests for AngularJS applications. It serves as an integrated solution that combines powerful tools and technologies, such as Node.js, Selenium WebDriver, Jasmine, Cucumber, and Mocha.

You can find more information about Protractor at `https://github.com/angular/protractor`. Jasmine is also compatible with Protractor because all the resources that are extracted from the browser to perform the tests are promises. Also, the `expect()` function of Jasmine internally handles these promises and makes it seem transparent validations tests.

However, the MEAN.JS generator does not have Protractor in its default installation. So, let's add the necessary dependencies to begin the test with this powerful framework. Perform the following steps:

1. Open your terminal in the root project folder and type the following command:

   `npm install protractor -save-dev`

2. In the `grunt-protractor-runner` folder, open the `node_modules/protractor/bin/webdriver-manager` file in your terminal and type the following command:

   `update`

 Don't forget the path `grunt-protractor-runner/node_modules/protractor/bin/webdriver-manager`; we'll be using it later in the chapter to run the Selenium server.

Now, let's create a Protractor configuration file in the root project folder using the following steps:

1. Add the `protractor.conf.js` file and place the following code; this is a good boilerplate to start working with Protractor on your AngularJS projects:

   ```
   // Protractor configuration
   // https://github.com/angular/protractor/blob/master/
   referenceConf.js

   'use strict';

   exports.config = {
       // The timeout for each script run on the browser.
       This should be longer
       // than the maximum time your application needs to
       stabilize between tasks.
       allScriptsTimeout: 110000,

       /**
   ```

```
* Use `seleniumAddress` for faster startup;
run `./node_modules/.bin/webdriver-manager start` to
launch the Selenium server.
* Use `seleniumPort` to let Protractor manage its own
Selenium server instance (using the server JAR in its
default location).
*/
seleniumAddress: 'http://localhost:4444/wd/hub',
// seleniumPort: 4444,


// A base URL for your application under test. Calls to
protractor.get()
// with relative paths will be prepended with this.
baseUrl: 'http://localhost:' + (process.env.PORT ||
'3000'),

// If true, only chromedriver will be started, not a standalone
selenium.
// Tests for browsers other than chrome will not run.
chromeOnly: false,

//chromeDriver: 'node_modules/grunt-protractor-
runner/node_modules/protractor/node_modules/selenium-
webdriver/chromedriver',

// list of files / patterns to load in the browser
specs: [
    'e2e/**/*.spec.js'
],

// Patterns to exclude.
exclude: [],

// ----- Capabilities to be passed to the webdriver instance
----
//
// For a full list of available capabilities, see
// https://code.google.com/p/selenium/wiki/
DesiredCapabilities
// and
// https://code.google.com/p/selenium/source/browse/
javascript/webdriver/capabilities.js
capabilities: {
```

```
    'browserName': 'chrome'
  },

  // ----- The test framework -----
  //
  // Jasmine and Cucumber are fully supported as a test and
  assertion framework.
  // Mocha has limited beta support. You will need to
  include your own
  // assertion framework if working with mocha.
  framework: 'jasmine',

  // ----- Options to be passed to minijasminenode -----
  //
  // See the full list at
  https://github.com/juliemr/minijasminenode
  jasmineNodeOpts: {
    defaultTimeoutInterval: 30000
  }
};
```

As a very well-documented file, we don't need deep analysis of every line, but the highlighted code has some important information about the `SeleniumAddress` instance generated, when we run the `webdriver` manager later in the chapter.

2. Let's add the `protractor` task to our `Gruntfile`; just add the following line right after the Karma task:

```
protractor: {
  options: {
    configFile: 'protractor.conf.js'
  },
  chrome: {
    options: {
      args: {
        browser: 'chrome'
      }
    }
  }
}
```

3. Add the following code right after the build task at the end in the
   Gruntfile.js file:

```
// Test task.
grunt.registerTask('test', ['env:test', 'mochaTest',
'karma:unit', 'protractor']);
```

The initial setup is done, but we need to create the test files. Let's see what we need
to do now.

Configuring the e2e testing folder

Let's add the e2e test folder to the root project. Perform the following steps:

1. Add an e2e folder to the root application folder.

2. Add a main folder inside the e2e folder.

3. Add a blank file called main.po.js.

4. Add another blank file called main.spec.js.

The e2e directory tests should be similar to the following screenshot:

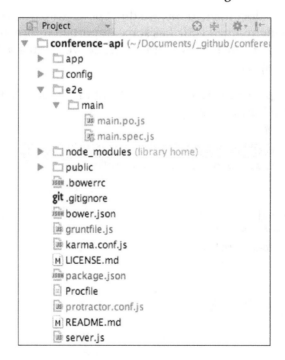

Now, let's add content to the `main.po.js` and `main.spec.js` files using the following steps:

1. Open the `main.po.js` file from the `e2e/main` folder and add the following lines of code:

```
'use strict';

var MainPage = function() {
  // Get UI elements to test
  this.heroEl = element(by.css('.jumbotron'));
  this.h1El = this.heroEl.element(by.css('h1'));
  this.anchorEl = this.heroEl.element(by.css('a'));

  this.repeater = by.repeater('speaker in speakers');
  this.speakerListCount =
  element.all(this.repeater).count();
};

module.exports = new MainPage();
```

Here, we just get some UI elements and a loop on the speaker object using the `repeater` feature.

 More information about the Protractor API and the repeater method can be found at `http://angular.github.io/protractor/#/api?view=ProtractorBy.prototype.repeater`.

2. Now, let's add content to `main.spec.js` from the `e2e/main` folder. Copy the following code and place it in the `main.spec.js` file:

```
'use strict';

describe('Main View', function() {
  var page;

  beforeEach(function() {
    browser.get('/');
    page = require('./main.po');
  });
```

```
// First test
it('should include conference name with call to action',
function() {
  // First Assertion - expect a text equal Conference
  expect(page.h1El.getText()).toBe('Conference');
  // Second Assertion - expect a anchor tag with Call for
  Papers text
  expect(page.anchorEl.getText()).toBe('Call for
  Papers');
  // Third Assertion - expect the url from Call for
  Papers link
  expect(page.anchorEl.getAttribute
  ('href')).toBe('http://localhost:3000/#!/signup');
});

// Second test
it('should render speakerList', function() {
  // First Assertion - expect a speaker list with
  6 speakers
  page.speakerListCount.then(function(count) {
    expect(count).toBe(6);
  });
});
});
```

Again, the code comments provide a necessary understanding for us to proceed with testing. Note that the UI elements captured in main.po.js are present here and each one has an expected behavior. The tests are simple and have enough information for large-scale SPA testing.

Starting the Selenium server

Well, we have already seen all the necessary steps to configure the Protractor test environment. Let's just start with the Selenium server and run tests. Perform the following steps:

1. Open the terminal and go to the path: grunt-protractor-runner/node_ modules/protractor/bin/ and type the following command:

    webdriver-manager start

    The command will start the Selenium server, and we are ready to start the tests. It's very important to run the application before proceeding with e2e testing! Don't forget to run the server.

2. Open the terminal in the root folder and type the following code:

```
node server
```

3. In the terminal, type the following command to start the tests:

```
grunt protractor
```

After running the tests, we can see the result on the terminal:

```
Running "protractor:chrome" (protractor) task
Using the selenium server at http://localhost:4444/wd/hub
. .

Finished in 11.643 seconds
2 tests, 4 assertions, 0 failures


Done, without errors.
```

Note that the tests were performed in the Chrome browser, as we configured the Grunt task in Chrome.

Let's add another browser to Gruntfile.js using the following steps:

1. Add the following highlighted code to the protractor task in gruntfile.js:

```
protractor: {
  options: {
    configFile: 'protractor.conf.js'
  },
  chrome: {
    options: {
      args: {
        browser: 'chrome'
      }
    }
  },
  safari: {
    options: {
      args: {
        browser: 'safari'
      }
    }
  }
}
```

2. Run the test again and let's see the result.

3. In the terminal, type the following command to start the tests:

```
grunt protractor
```

The following screenshot illustrates the final result that runs the tests on two browsers:

```
Running "protractor:chrome" (protractor) task
Using the selenium server at http://localhost:4444/wd/hub
. .


Finished in 11.093 seconds
2 tests, 4 assertions, 0 failures


Running "protractor:safari" (protractor) task
Using the selenium server at http://localhost:4444/wd/hub
. .


Finished in 12.506 seconds
2 tests, 4 assertions, 0 failures


Done, without errors.
```

The framework will test each browser configured in the Gruntfile.js file. However, remember that you need to have the browser installed on your workstation to perform the tests.

As you can see, the browser opens quickly, runs the test, and closes.

Summary

This was a very long chapter focused on tests; we saw how to perform unit testing on SPA. We also saw some testing frameworks to facilitate our work.

You learned how to perform tests on AngularJS applications using the Protractor framework and the Selenium server. Remember that you should thoroughly test your applications to avoid future problems as the source code grows.

In the next chapter, we will see how to put SPA in production in the cloud service. We will also see some interesting points about SPAs and its scalability.

8
Deploying the Application to the Cloud

We've now reached the final stage of development of our sample SPA. In this chapter, we will look at some important points involving all processes of web applications, such as version control, deployment in the cloud, and continuous application deployment. We will cover the following topics:

- Hosting the project on GitHub
- Continuous application deployment
- Automatic deployment from GitHub
- Hands-on deployment
- Some final notes about SPA

Hosting the project on GitHub

Before we proceed with the deployment to the cloud, we need to review some important points in our sample application. As mentioned earlier, we need to host our source code on `http://github.com`. Since we already use Git as our version control system, uploading our code to the GitHub service is very simple.

Git is a powerful version control system and has many GUI clients for Windows and Mac OS X. If you are on Mac OS X, we recommend the use of `https://mac.github.com/` and for Windows users `https://windows.github.com/`; both are free tools.

In the following examples, we are using terminal; to have the Git commands available on terminal, you need to install Git on your system.

You can find more information on how to install Git at the following URL: http://git-scm.com/.

As we already have everything configured, we just need to commit the last changes with the following command:

```
git commit -m"refactoring adding Protractor testing Framework"
```

Now we need a GitHub account to host our source code. If you already have one, go straight to step 13.

1. Open your browser and go to www.github.com to create your free account. After the registration process, you will be redirected to the home screen; now it's time to create a repository to store the source code.

2. Click on the plus (+) sign to the right of your username and click on **New repository** in the pop-up menu, as shown in the following screenshot:

3. You need to give a name and description to the new repository. Type the name and description as shown in the following screenshot:

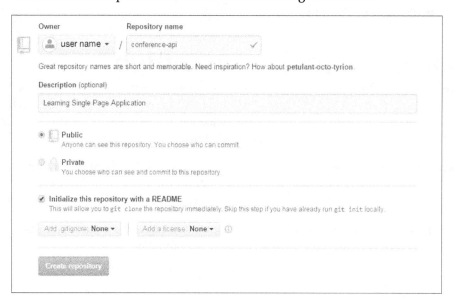

You can find more about starting with GitHub at
`https://help.github.com/articles/create-a-repo/`.

4. Now it's time to configure the connection between Git and GitHub. To do this, open your Git shell application. Type the following command into the Git shell:

   ```
   git config --global user.name "YOUR NAME"
   git config --global user.email "YOUR EMAIL ADDRESS"
   ```

   Both commands' servers inform GitHub who are you and print your name on each commit you made.

5. The next step is to configure an SSH key between your computer and the GitHub repository. Type the following command into your Git shell:

   ```
   ssh-keygen -t rsa -C "your_email@example.com"
   ```

6. Replace the default e-mail address with your own e-mail address and follow the instructions on the Git shell. Next, you'll be asked to enter a passphrase.

7. You will see something similar to the following result:

   ```
   Your identification has been saved in /c/Users/you/.ssh/id_rsa.
   # Your public key has been saved in /c/Users/you/.ssh/id_rsa.pub.
   # The key fingerprint is:
   # 01:0f:f4:3b:ca:85:d6:17:a1:7d:f0:68:9d:f0:a2:db your_email@
   example.com
   ```

8. Then add your new key to `ssh-agent`:

   ```
   ssh-agent -s
   ssh-add ~/.ssh/id_rsa
   ```

9. Now it is time to place the key on your GitHub account, so type the following command into the Git shell to copy the key:

   ```
   clip < ~/.ssh/id_rsa.pub
   ```

10. Go back to your GitHub account and click on the settings tool to the right of your username.

11. On the users side bar, click on **SSH Keys** and add the SSH keys.

12. Paste your key inside the Key input field.

    With this step, we have finished setting up your computer and the GitHub account with secure SSH keys.

13. One last action is required: testing to make sure everything works.

14. Open your Git shell and type the following command:

```
ssh -T git@github.com
```

You may see the following output:

```
The authenticity of host 'github.com (207.97.227.239)' can't be
established.
# RSA key fingerprint is 16:27:ac:a5:76:28:2d:36:63:1b:56:4d:eb:df
:a6:48.
# Are you sure you want to continue connecting (yes/no)?
```

15. Confirm the message and check the output message; you should have something like the following:

```
Hi username! You've successfully authenticated, but GitHub does
not
# provide shell access.
```

This message indicates success.

16. After that, upload the following code to the repository:

```
git push origin master
```

 All source code of the project can be found at https://github. com/newaeonweb/conference-api. There are four prereleases and a final release.

To follow the next examples, you can download the 0.0.4 release at https://github.com/newaeonweb/conference-api/releases/tag/0.0.4. This contains the commits from the last chapter where we implemented Protractor for e2e testing.

GitHub is a great alternative to store the version control of the source code in a safe place.

It's free for open source projects and is used by many companies. Moreover, it is highly integrated with several other web platforms, as discussed in the following section on continuous integration and automated builds.

Continuous application development

As developers, we often work in teams, and to keep our sanity, we need a control version, some good development practices, and automated processes.

The term **continuous application development** came from continuous software development and other terms such as continuous integration, continuous delivery, continuous testing, and continuous deployment. These terms cover many aspects of the application development process in agile methodologies.

With this in mind, we can use some tools that make our work simpler, like a continuous integration services.

Continuous integration is a term that originated in agile methodology and **Extreme programming** (**XP**), and means something simple: the developer of one team integrates the code for the main project at the same frequency as new features are developed by another team. This process is done many times a day for both teams. So the main purpose of using continuous integration is to integrate the new features and changes made by teams to the existing project without breaking the application.

Each code commit is tested and deployed into production as soon as it is available and the process is automated. As a crucial part in the development process and for the success of continuous integration, version control should be used. This is the main reason why we chose Git and GitHub since one of the goals of version control is collaborative work in which several developers work together with the same source code.

Version control is essential for every development methodology, and a good continuous integration tool is essential to have continuous development. For this reason, we have adopted a tool called Shippable, which can integrate our GitHub account and automate the entire build process and testing. In addition, we can put our application directly into production at the end of the build.

 More information can be found at the Shippable website at `http://www.shippable.com/`.

Shippable is a continuous delivery cloud service. Through it, we can do several types of integration, run tests, compile, build, and put our application directly into production. As well as all of these advantages, it naturally integrates with our application. In the next section, we will see how to deploy directly from our account on GitHub.

Automatic deployment from GitHub

As already mentioned, in agile development at the end of each delivery, or sprint as it is regularly called, we need to put the application into production. Now we will see how to do this in an automated manner.

The following lines assume you have already configured a local repository using Git and a GitHub account.

Setting up a Shippable account

Setting up an account on Shippable is very simple and is free. Moreover, you can use your account on GitHub or Bitbucket.

1. Visit `http://www.shippable.com/` and click on the **github** button. Then follow the instructions to register.

    After the authorization process between GitHub and Shippable, you'll be redirected to the Shippable dashboard.

2. On the right-hand side, click on your account name right below **Organizations** as shown in the following screenshot:

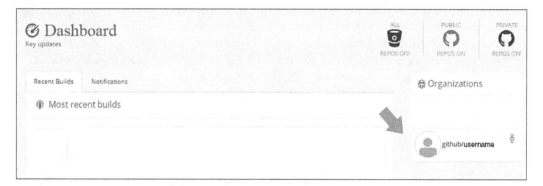

3. Then click on the repository name's link.
4. Enable your GitHub repository.

Very simple so far!

 Do not forget to choose the repository that stores our sample application.

At this point, you have probably noticed that it is possible to run the application directly from the dashboard by clicking on the play symbol in the actions column. However, it is not the time to run the application yet. We still need to follow some steps to correctly set up the environment.

Let's now set up another free service: this time, Heroku hosting.

Setting up a Heroku account

Heroku is a cloud service platform, PaaS, that supports multiple programming languages. It is one of the oldest cloud services and started its activities supporting only the Ruby language. Setting up an account is pretty simple: just go to `https://id.heroku.com/signup` and follow the registration steps.

After the registration process, follow these steps:

1. On the dashboard, click on the plus (**+**) sign to create a new app and choose a name (we chose **conference-api**), as shown in the following screenshot:

Before we proceed, we still need to perform some actions, so let's go back to the Shippable dashboard.

2. On your dashboard, click on **Organizations** and the GitHub account name, as shown in the following screenshot:

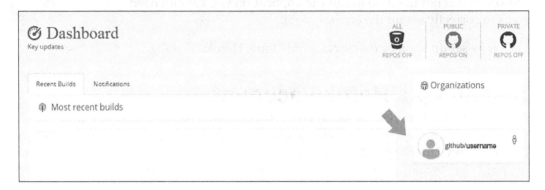

3. Now we need to get the SSH key, so click on **Deployment Key** and copy the ssh-rsa key, as shown in the following screenshot:

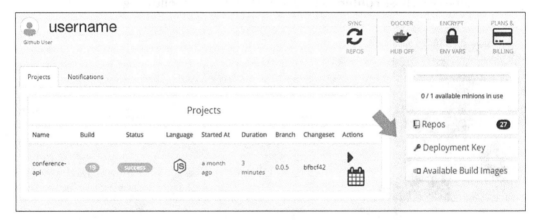

4. Go back to the Heroku dashboard and click on your account name, then click on the **Manage Account** menu item, as shown in the following screenshot:

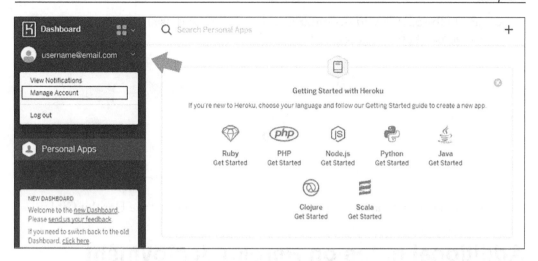

5. Go to **SSH Keys** at the bottom of the Account page and click on the **Edit** button in the right-hand corner, as shown in the following screenshot:

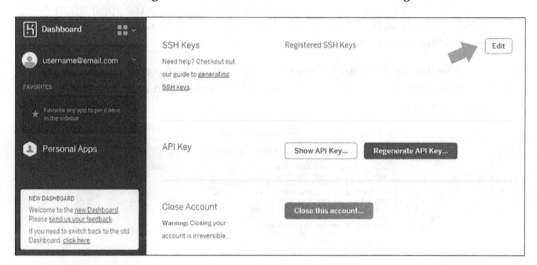

6. Paste the SSH key in the **enter new key** input field as shown in the following screenshot and click on the **Save** button.

7. Go back to the dashboard and go to Settings, and copy the Heroku Git URL.

Additional notes on Heroku deployment

In the examples given throughout the book, we are utilizing a process of deployment that is widely used in web software development, through a continuous integration service (Shippable). However, you can proceed with deploying the application directly from your local development environment to a cloud service or even to your own hosting service using Heroku Toolbelt.

Heroku Toolbelt is a command-line program that lets you use specific commands in your terminal as: `heroku help`. The result of this command is shown in the following screenshot:

```
Usage: heroku COMMAND [--app APP] [command-specific-options]

Primary help topics, type "heroku help TOPIC" for more details:

  addons     #  manage addon resources
  apps       #  manage apps (create, destroy)
  auth       #  authentication (login, logout)
  config     #  manage app config vars
  domains    #  manage custom domains
  logs       #  display logs for an app
  ps         #  manage dynos (dynos, workers)
  releases   #  manage app releases
  run        #  run one-off commands (console, rake)
  sharing    #  manage collaborators on an app

Additional topics:

  certs       #  manage ssl endpoints for an app
  drains      #  display syslog drains for an app
  fork        #  clone an existing app
  git         #  manage git for apps
  help        #  list commands and display help
  keys        #  manage authentication keys
  labs        #  manage optional features
  maintenance #  manage maintenance mode for an app
  members     #  manage membership in organization accounts
  orgs        #  manage organization accounts
  pg          #  manage heroku-postgresql databases
  pgbackups   #  manage backups of heroku postgresql databases
  plugins     #  manage plugins to the heroku gem
  regions     #  list available regions
  stack       #  manage the stack for an app
  status      #  check status of heroku platform
  twofactor   #
  update      #  update the heroku client
  version     #  display version
```

You can find more information about direct deployment in the Heroku documentation at `https://devcenter.heroku.com/articles/git`.

After this brief explanation about direct deployment, we have finished the configuration steps on Shippable and Heroku, so let's go back to the application's code.

Hands-on deployment

Since we're using the MEAN.JS generator, we have a file available in the application root folder named `.travis.yml`. We can use it for the initial setup on Shippable; however, we will create a new file.

 Travis is another tool for continuous integration in open source projects, which is directly integrated with GitHub. More information is available at `http://docs.travis-ci.com/`.

To create the file, follow these steps:

1. Open the project and add a new file in the root folder named `.shippable.yml`.
2. Paste the following code and save the file:

```
language: node_jsnode_js:
  - "0.10"
env:
  - NODE_ENV=travis
services:
  - mongodb
after_success:
  - git push git@heroku.com:<some name>.git master
```

The last command in this file, `after_success`, receives the Git Heroku URL that was copied in step 7 of the *Setting up a Heroku account* section. After all the commands have run successfully, this line confirms the automatic deployment. However, one last action is required, that is, adding another file to the root folder.

3. Create a new file called `Procfile` in the root project folder and type the following code in it:

```
web: ./node_modules/.bin/forever -m 5 server.js
```

`Procfile` determines which specific commands must be executed by your application dynos on the Heroku platform. These commands can vary for several types of processes such as: web, worker, urgentworker, and clock, among others.

 You can find more about the Heroku process at `https://devcenter.heroku.com/articles/procfile`.

That's all, so let's commit and upload the changes to Git and push them to the GitHub repository.

Checking the build process

In the Shippable dashboard, it is possible to view all the builds performed, and it is also possible to identify errors and monitor the entire process, as shown in the following screenshot:

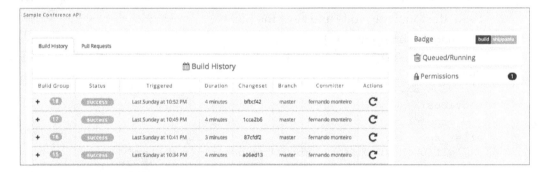

We have a detailed log showing step by step the running process. It is possible to consult the log for each of the builds performed as shown in the following screenshot:

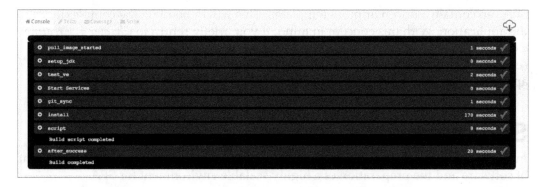

Checking the application in production

After completing all of these processes, the application will be available at
`http://<the name you give before>.herokuapp.com/`. Open your browser
and visit the application in production. The example application can be found at
`http://conference-api.herokuapp.com`.

Final notes on SPA

Finally, we would like to emphasize some important points that were discussed
throughout the book.

The term SPA refers to a main container that carries several templates within itself;
something very similar to the concept of master pages in the .NET framework.
The following figure illustrates the main difference between SPA and a traditional
web application.

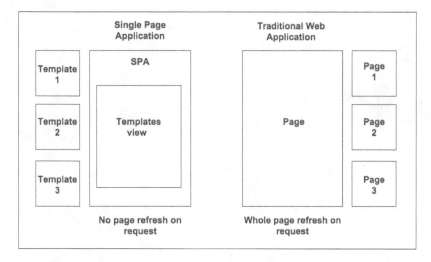

SPA can contain a dozen or more templates. This will depend on the complexity of the application. With this concept in mind, if you briefly return to *Chapter 4, Creating a Conference Web Application,* you can see that we wrote SPA that only ran on the server side, even using an API, much like the traditional way to build dynamic applications in server-side languages such as PHP and .NET.

Summary

In this chapter, we discussed some factors of extreme importance to the development of software and the preparation of a highly scalable environment for SPA.

With the process of testing an automatic build, we can deploy the application in minutes and ensure a quality delivery. We covered many important concepts and tools for the frontend development of SPA with the RESTful API. This entire book serves as a solid base for learning not only about SPA but also depicts examples and tips about MEAN development and the RESTful architecture, covering a complete approach to the whole development process of SPA.

Index

M

MEAN.io
about 53, 54
versus MEAN.JS 126
MEAN.JS
about 53, 54
URL 53, 126
versus MEAN.io 126
MEAN.JS generator
about 125, 126
dissecting 125, 126
URL 131
MEAN stack
about 19, 20
generators 23, 24
task manager 23, 24
tools, debugging 23
tools, for developing web applications 20
middleware 32, 33
Mocha
URL 165
model
creating, Mongoose schema used 65, 66
Model, AngularJS 109, 110
Model View Controller (MVC) 10
Model View Presenter (MVP) 10
Model View ViewModel (MVVM) 10
module.exports object 38
module_name npm update command 33
modules, AngularJS
about 118
URL 118
MongoDB
about 20, 31, 40
and terminal 40
connection, with Mongoose 45
Mongoose models 45-47
Mongoose schemas 45-47
mongo shell 42-44
relational database, comparing with
    NoSQL database 41
URL 20
used, in cloud 69, 70
MongoDB commands
versus SQL commands 42

Mongoose
models 45-47
MongoDB connection, using with 45
schemas 45-47
Mongoose schema
used, for creating model 65, 66
mongo shell 42-44
MVC pattern 11-14
MV* pattern 11-15
MVVM pattern
about 11-15
Model 13
URL 13
View 13
ViewModel 13
working 14

N

ng-app property 108
ng-repeat directive 134
Node.js
URL 32
Node module
about 37, 38, 118
using 37, 38
working with 35
Node module, variables
__dirname 38
__filename 38
process 38
process.argv 38
process.env 39
process.stderr 38
process.stdin 38
process.stout 38
require.main 39
Node Package Manager (NPM) 21, 32, 33
Node server
about 32, 33
with server.js 64
node server command 77, 132
NoSQL database
advantages 42
relational database, comparing with 41
npm adduser username command 33

npm install module_name command 33
npm install module_name-save
    command 33
npm list command 33
npm list-g command 33
npm publish command 33
npm remove module_name command 33
NPM repository
    URL 32
npm -v command 33
npm whoami command 33

O

Object Data Mapping (ODM) 45
Object Relational Mapping (ORM) 45

P

Package Control
    URL 22
package.json file
    creating 60
    initiating 60-63
Passport middleware
    adding 84-87
    changes, reviewing in server.js file 90
    password encryption, adding 88, 89
    password encryption, setting to
        user model 89
    session control, adding 88, 89
    URL 87
Passport module 55, 56
password encryption
    adding 88, 89
    setting, to user model 89
Platform as a Service (PaaS) 69
PM
    about 11
    URL 12
Postman
    data, inserting with 71-74
Presenter 15
profile page
    creating 99-105
project
    hosting, on GitHub 175-178

project organization 119-122
Protractor API
    URL 171
Protractor (e2e testing)
    configuring 166-169
    e2e testing folder, configuring 170-172
    Selenium server, starting 172-174
    URL 167
public folder 129
Pure CSS
    about 28-30
    URL 28
    used, for frontend views 98

R

Read-Eval-Print Loop (REPL) 36
relational database
    comparing, with NoSQL database 41
repeater method
    URL 171
require() function
    about 35-37
    working with 35
Responsive Boilerplate
    about 29
    URL 28
    used, for frontend views 98
res.render() function 93
root folder
    .bowerrec 130
    .gitignore 130
    bower.json 130
    gruntfile.js 130
    karma.conf.js 130
    license.md 130
    package.json 130
    procfile 131
    readme.md 131
    server.js 131
routes
    /api/speakers 66
    /api/speakers/:speaker_id 66
    dealing with 93-95
    defining, to CRUD functions 66-69

W

WebStorm
  about 21
  Karma, testing with 165, 166
  URL 21
Windows Presentation
     Foundation (WPF) 12

Y

Yeoman
  about 24, 56
  URL 24, 56

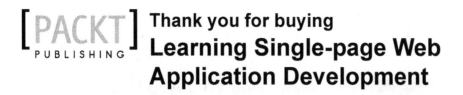

Thank you for buying
Learning Single-page Web Application Development

About Packt Publishing

Packt, pronounced 'packed', published its first book, *Mastering phpMyAdmin for Effective MySQL Management*, in April 2004, and subsequently continued to specialize in publishing highly focused books on specific technologies and solutions.

Our books and publications share the experiences of your fellow IT professionals in adapting and customizing today's systems, applications, and frameworks. Our solution-based books give you the knowledge and power to customize the software and technologies you're using to get the job done. Packt books are more specific and less general than the IT books you have seen in the past. Our unique business model allows us to bring you more focused information, giving you more of what you need to know, and less of what you don't.

Packt is a modern yet unique publishing company that focuses on producing quality, cutting-edge books for communities of developers, administrators, and newbies alike. For more information, please visit our website at www.packtpub.com.

Writing for Packt

We welcome all inquiries from people who are interested in authoring. Book proposals should be sent to author@packtpub.com. If your book idea is still at an early stage and you would like to discuss it first before writing a formal book proposal, then please contact us; one of our commissioning editors will get in touch with you.

We're not just looking for published authors; if you have strong technical skills but no writing experience, our experienced editors can help you develop a writing career, or simply get some additional reward for your expertise.

Mastering Web Application Development with AngularJS

ISBN: 978-1-78216-182-0   Paperback: 372 pages

Build single-page web applications using the power of AngularJS

1. Make the most out of AngularJS by understanding the AngularJS philosophy and applying it to real-life development tasks.

2. Effectively structure, write, test, and finally deploy your application.

3. Add security and optimization features to your AngularJS applications.

HTML5 Web Application Development By Example

ISBN: 978-1-84969-594-7   Paperback: 276 pages

Learn how to build rich, interactive web applications from the ground up using HTML5, CSS3, and jQuery

1. Packed with example applications that show you how to create rich, interactive applications and games.

2. Shows you how to use the most popular and widely supported features of HTML5.

3. Full of tips and tricks for writing more efficient and robust code while avoiding some of the pitfalls inherent to JavaScript.

Express Web Application Development

ISBN: 978-1-84969-654-8   Paperback: 236 pages

Learn how to develop web applications with the Express framework from scratch

1. Exploring all aspects of web development using the Express framework.

2. Starts with the essentials.

3. Expert tips and advice covering all Express topics.

Node Web Development
Second Edition

ISBN: 978-1-78216-330-5   Paperback: 248 pages

A practical introduction to Node.js, an exciting server-side JavaScript web development stack

1. Learn about server-side JavaScript with Node.js and Node modules.

2. Website development both with and without the Connect/Express web application framework.

3. Developing both HTTP server and client applications.

Please check **www.PacktPub.com** for information on our titles